THE LINGUISTICS OF PUNCTUATION

C S L I
Lecture Notes
Number 18

THE
LINGUISTICS
OF
PUNCTUATION

Geoffrey Nunberg

CENTER FOR THE STUDY
OF LANGUAGE
AND INFORMATION

CSLI was founded early in 1983 by researchers from Stanford University, SRI International, and Xerox PARC to further research and development of integrated theories of language, information, and computation. CSLI headquarters and the publication offices are located at the Stanford site.

CSLI/SRI International   CSLI/Stanford   CSLI/Xerox PARC
333 Ravenswood Ave.   Ventura Hall   3333 Coyote Hill Rd.
Menlo Park, CA 94025   Stanford, CA 94305   Palo Alto, CA 94304

Library of Congress Cataloging-in-Publication Data
Nunberg, Geoffrey, 1945–
      The linguistics of punctuation / Geoffrey Nunberg.
        p.   cm. — (CSLI lecture notes : no. 18)
      Includes bibliographical references.
      Includes index.
      ISBN 0-937073-47-4. — ISBN 0-937073-46-6 (pbk.)
      1. English language — Punctuation.   I. Title. II. Series.
PE 1450.N78 1990
421'.52–dc20   90-1411
                                       CIP

For Sophie

ACKNOWLEDGEMENTS

In preparing this monograph, I have benefitted from the helpful comments of many colleagues, including Curtis Abbott, Mike Dixon, Jeff Goldberg, John Lamping, Joan Levinson, Bob Newsom, Brian Smith, and Tayloe Stansbury. For their comments on earlier drafts of this work, I am also grateful to Jim McCawley, Peter Sells, Susan Stucky, Tom Wasow, and Annie Zaenen. For help in preparation of this manuscript, I am extremely indebted to Susi Lilly.

TABLE OF CONTENTS

1 Introduction: In Search of the Written Language

Linguists have always approached the study of writing contrastively, as a mode of linguistic expression alternative to speech. For a long time, the contrast was drawn primarily in order to deprecate or dismiss writing as an object of theoretical interest. As Bloomfield famously put it, "Writing is not language, but merely a means of recording language by means of visual marks." More recently, the tendency has been to regard writing and speech as distinct linguistic systems. But even so, the written language – that is, the system of figural representation that is of particular linguistic interest – is still defined and legitimated by reference to the properties of the spoken language. Most notably, the adequacy of the written language is assessed, one way or the other, according to how it makes available the same kinds of expressive devices as spoken varieties. To the extent that the written language measures up, it is regarded as expressively equivalent to spoken language, and thus (by an argument that is somewhat cloudy in its details), as worthy of serious linguistic study.[1] Hence the tendency in recent work has been to try to assimi-

---

[1]The arguments offered by both sides suffer from several basic conceptual confusions. In the first place, they rely on an unwarranted assumption that the representation relation is not transitive: that if A represents B and B represents C, A cannot be a representation of C. By this argument we would have to conclude that a photograph of a painting of Charles II cannot serve as a representation of Charles II, a point we might be unwilling to grant. (I

late the differences between writing and speech to the differences between spoken varieties. As Sampson (1985:27) writes: "The kind of English that we use in writing and the kind we use in speech are, in the linguist's technical sense, closely-related dialects . . . ."

This contrastive approach has militated against the development of the autonomous study of written language as a linguistic system in its own right. (By contrast, the subject of writing *systems* is well established as a domain of study.) Indeed, current approaches to writing presuppose that there couldn't be much to say about the subject. In order to defend the legitimacy of the study of written language, linguists have gone to some lengths to argue that, as Biber (1986:385) puts it, "few (if any) absolute differences exist between speech and writing." What distinguishes the two varieties, on the current view, is predominantly the pervasive differences in the circumstances of their production, processing, and social and communicative functions. These differences may leave their mark on the written language primarily in the relative frequency with which various types of expressions and constructions are used in each variety, as documented in a growing literature.[2] But none of these

---

have adapted this example from Smith (1987), who discusses a number of these issues in detail.) In fact the relations of correspondence and representation that hold between writing and speech are a good deal more subtle than writers on the topic have realized. I will touch on these in the discussion of the relation between punctuation and intonation below, but they are really deserving of independent treatment. Note, however, that there is no rational grounds for linking questions about the representational status of writing to its interest as an area of research. Writing could be a derivative mode of representation and yet have an interest of its own; or it could be independent and a bore.

[2]See, e.g., Kroch and Hindle (1982), Chafe (1982), Chafe and Danielewicz (1985) and Biber (1986). In the typical study, an analyst tabulates the relative frequency in writing and speech of a given construction (say topicalization, *it*-cleft or passive), and proceeds to argue that the skewings can be explained by invoking differences in the contexts or communicative functions that are characteristically associated with the use of each medium. In more recent studies, analysts have refined this approach to take into account the gradience of the dimensions along which written and spoken varieties are arrayed, by further classifying types of communication according to their

observations have suggested the existence of any essential qualitative difference between written and spoken language.

Taken at face value, this would be a more interesting claim than linguists sometimes seem to realize. It should no longer be necessary to defend the view that writing is *truly* language, but it is surprising to learn that it is *merely* language. After all, intellectualized written languages like English are the result of a process of standardization and specialization that has been going on for at least four hundred years, during which time spoken and written varieties have led largely disparate lives – learned in different ways and at different stages of life, used in different media and different contexts to communicate different information for different purposes to different audiences. Under the circumstances, we might expect that written language would emerge with certain structural and representational features that were unique to that mode.

On examination, however, the arguments that linguists offer for the equivalence of written and spoken language do not really address this broader question. For the most part, they have relied on the observation that the two varieties appear to make available the same sorts of lexical and syntactic resources, in particular those that have figured prominently in analyses of the structure of the spoken language: for example, that constructions like topicalization (as in *This book, everyone has read*), clefting (*It is this book that everyone has read*), passive and so on appear in both written and spoken varieties. This observation may be adequate to support the claim that written language is not defective as a linguistic system, but by itself it does not demonstrate that there are therefore no interesting systematic lexical or syntactic differences between the varieties. For one thing, the point is based primarily on observations about the raw distribution of forms in one or another variety. But the fact that a form *appears* in one or the other mode does not entail that it *belongs* to that mode. Both writing and speech are, after all, extremely versatile: when it comes to the crunch, there are few if any features of

---

degree of formality, their genre and topic, their intended audience, and so forth.

spoken language that cannot be at least approximately transcribed in certain written texts (say in reporting dialogue) and conversely, very few features of the written language that cannot be rendered in reading aloud. (Thus the fact that we can say "quote. . . unquote" does not mean that there is a single device for direct quotation that is shared by the varieties.)[3]

But even if writing is capable of expressing all of the relevant or important features of the spoken language, we are still left with the question of deciding whether there is anything *more* to the written language than the features it shares with speech. The contrastive approach makes it difficult to consider those features of written texts that have no obvious analogues in speech, or whose spoken-

---

[3]It is true that many of the qualitative differences between written and spoken varieties can appropriately be laid to dialect or register differences. It is a well-established fact that written varieties tend to be more conservative than spoken ones: forms often survive in the written language long after they become obsolete in speech, and new forms may become common in the spoken language without ever making their way into the written standard. But there are other differences that cannot be dismissed in this way. One example (for which I am grateful to Tom Wasow) involves the use of inversion in comparatives, as in *They were more reluctant than were their friends*, which presents a counter-example to the universal which Emonds (1976) described in terms of restrictions on the operation of "root" transformations in subordinate clauses. One might find such constructions in formal spoken style, of course, but it is possible to ask whether they could exist there if they were not essentially assigned to the written variety, which could involve a somewhat different sort of parsing (or generative) mechanism, and so which may not be responsible to exactly the same set of syntactic constraints as the spoken variety.

In a different domain, we note that contrastive studies of writing and speech have paid very little attention to systems of deixis and indexicals, perhaps because these are not yet amenable to a canonical description in the theoretical apparatus available for spoken language. (Though in this connection, see Fillmore (1975), Rubin (1980).) For example, certain deictics are peculiar to the written language, such as "the above"; whereas other deictics acquire specialized uses in writing: *now* means "at this point in the text"; *here* means "in this text"; *elsewhere* means "in another publication"; and so on. These observations are in fact the tip of a substantial theoretical iceberg, which we will touch on again in the discussion of parentheticals in Chapter 6 below.

language analogues are either theoretically marginal or poorly understood. In particular, linguists have almost wholly ignored the graphical circumstances of the written language, and have had very little to say about the relation of the written language to the various systems of figural conventions that figure along with the inscriptions of lexical content in the construction and interpretation of texts.

In a typical book, for example, written lexical expressions are presented in concert with punctuation marks; with the two-dimensional schemes of presentation that are used in lists, tables and diagrams; with the varieties of non-linear indexing systems exploited in the use of footnotes, tables of contents and textual cross-references; with the format- and font-alternations that announce paragraphs, titles, section headings and the like; and with a number of other figural and graphical devices. It can of course be argued that many of these conventions are not part of the written language itself, but instead belong to collateral systems of graphical representation associated with the presentation of written-language documents, and so are not matters of particular linguistic concern. But that argument has to be made on principled grounds.

Consider how much attention has been given to the analogous problems that arise in every domain of linguistics when we try to identify and abstract the spoken language from among the facts of the utterances in which it is realized; for example, in fixing the boundary between phonetics and phonology; in separating the linguistic from the paralinguistic and gestural in discussions of intonation; or in sorting out the linguistic and extralinguistic contributions to phenomena like demonstrative reference. These discussions have invariably been vexed and subtle, involving such questions as the functions of the relevant features, the degree to which they exhibit the same kind of systematicity that is observed in other linguistic domains, and the degree to which their regularities can be derived by reference to independent non-linguistic principles. But notably, they have not involved appeals to the contrast with other modes: so far as I know, no one has tried to argue that intonation cannot be part of language because it is not fully represented in the written mode. In the figural domain, by contrast, contrastive definition is the only game in town: the written language is implicitly assumed to consist of whatever in the text can be read aloud.

In this monograph, I will be examining the graphical system that is most closely associated with the textual realization of written lexical expressions: the system of punctuation, or more accurately, the system of text-categories that punctuation, along with other graphical devices, is used to indicate. I will argue that punctuation is in fact a linguistic subsystem, and hence to be considered as part of the wider system of the written language, though its systematicity is apt to be obscured if we try to analyze it contrastively, by reference to the set of spoken-language devices with which it has some functional overlap.

It is not easy to say what makes a system "linguistic" in some privileged sense of a term that has only privileged senses. It is obviously not sufficient to show that punctuation can be described by a grammar, even one which is constrained along roughly the same lines as the grammars of natural spoken languages. And it would be futile to try to cash in the category of "language" in terms of any particular formal definition; to say, that is, that the grammar of text-category indicators shares just such-and-such a set of formal properties with natural-language syntax and phonology, in distinction to the grammars describing constructed languages or other non-linguistic systems of figural representation, and that these properties are criterial to the definition of the class of natural languages. For the present purposes, I will try to show only that the grammar of written-language text-category indicators has the "look and feel" of the grammars of other kinds of natural-language systems, and equally important, that the enterprise of analyzing such grammars has the look and feel of linguistic analysis. Thus it will be important to show that the rules of punctuation are at once more complex and more systematic than handbook expositions would suggest; that they are not accessible to casual introspection; and that they are organized along lines that suggest the influence of the principles of organization that underlie the structure of other natural-language systems, as opposed to the sorts of rational principles that people bring to bear when they set about designing artificial languages of various sorts. In particular, I want to show

how these rules are interdefined as elements of a single complex system, which imposes constraints on their application that transcend their individual functions.

From the historical perspective, the point can be made by saying that the system of text-category indicators is an *application* of natural language. By this I mean that the system has arisen through a kind of application of the principles of natural-language design, as a means of imposing a certain organization on the lexical content of written texts. Viewed as a whole, the system has no analogue in the spoken language (though certain of its functions overlap with those of various spoken-language devices). Rather, the system has arisen, in the course of written-language standardization and intellectualization, as a response to the particular communicative requirements of written language texts, and as an exploitation of the particular expressive resources that graphical presentation makes available. It is what follows, roughly, from setting language down.

The emergence of this system should be seen in the context of the wider process of development of specialized systems of graphical representation and of graphical devices for the presentation and integration of expressions of both natural and constructed languages. In this sense the "linguistics of writing" – that is, the study of written language as a system in its own right – is appropriately thought of as a part of the study of graphical representation in general. From this point of view, we want to have a descriptive apparatus for written natural language that enables us to contrast its structure with those of constructed languages of various sorts (for example, with systems of mathematical and musical representation), as well as with semi-linguistic and non-linguistic systems like those used for architectural rendering or graphs and diagrams of various sorts.[4]

---

[4]There has been some valuable programmatic work done in this area, though it has not yet reached the level of sophistication that linguistics makes available for the description of spoken natural languages. See, e.g., Mountford (1980), Norrish (1987).

2 ENGLISH PUNCTUATION: THE LIMITATIONS OF CONTRASTIVE APPROACHES

LINGUISTS ON PUNCTUATION

With few exceptions, the extensive literature on written language and writing systems has almost nothing to say about punctuation, from either a historical or theoretical point of view. There is little reason to revise the observation that Gleason (1965) made more than twenty years ago, to the effect that "no appreciable amount of research has ever been devoted to [questions of punctuation]. . . . Indeed, there is available very little descriptive data on how the English, or any other, punctuation system is actually used. The large volume of published material which is available is predominantly normative. . ."[5]

---

[5]This statement requires some qualification. There are a few quite good traditional descriptions of English punctuation, which I have consulted freely. For American punctuation, the most comprehensive guide is the Chicago *Manual of Style*; also useful are Sumney (1949) and Whitehall (1954). More recently, Meyer (1983, 1987) presents a useful and thorough survey of the use of American punctuation, based on a statistical analysis of material in the Brown corpus. Meyer's work tends to focus on the relation of punctuation to lexical structures, as opposed to those aspects of punctuation that enable us to see it as a system in its own right; it also suffers from a

There are various reasons for this neglect. For one thing, full-blown systems of punctuation are historically a relatively late development, and are not fully realized even in many well-established written-language traditions. While it is possible to trace the antecedents of modern English punctuation back to the English and Latin manuscript traditions, for example, it is not until well after the introduction of print that there appears anything like the standardized, elaborated and autonomous system of punctuation that is found in the public uses of intellectualized written languages like English or French. For this reason, the study of punctuation has been irrelevant to ongoing discussions about the origins of writing, or about the changes that the introduction of writing works on individual cognition and on the social order.[6]

---

limitation that often affects such statistical surveys, in considering only what does occur, and in failing to ask after the constraints that account for the non-occurrence of various sequences.

Partridge (1953) is the most thorough guide to modern British usage; also useful is Carey (1952). The Fowler's *The King's English* (1931 edition), though generally dated and impressionistic, gives what is still the most insightful overall discussion of the topic of punctuation, and rewards a careful and generous-minded reading.

Levinson (1986) is an excellent treatment of the historical development of punctuation systems up to the introduction of print (the point at which, from our point of view, the action gets interesting).

[6]By the same token, punctuation has been of little interest to linguists concerned with the practical problems of developing new orthographies to accommodate the phonological systems of hitherto unwritten languages, precisely because the rules of punctuation seem to be in large measure independent of language-specific features. Thus language planners do not have to devise a new system of punctuation as they do a new orthography: they can simply borrow the system already in place in other writing systems. It is fair to say, in fact, that there is only one system of punctuation (in the sense, at least, in which we would say there is only one Roman alphabet), which is used in all developed Western, alphabetic languages, subject to the fixing of a few parameters and the establishment of various local conventions and constraints.

Of course here, as in other areas of language, it is natural that handbook writers should pay particular attention to cross-linguistic differences (for

Most importantly, the topic of punctuation has suffered from the contrastive approach that has dominated the study of writing, which requires that we characterize the features of the written language by reference to some analogous features of the spoken language. Thus punctuation is usually regarded as a (highly imperfect and limited) device for transcribing certain of the prosodic and pausal features of speech. As Markwardt (1942) put it: "Punctuation is in large part a system of conventions the function of which is to assist the written language in indicating those elements of speech which cannot be conveniently set down on paper: chiefly pause, pitch, and stress."

Seen in this light, punctuation is uninteresting for two reasons. First, the intonational features that punctuation is assumed to represent are themselves notoriously difficult to describe, and have traditionally been assigned a marginal role with respect to the rest of the linguistic system of the spoken language (so much so that they are often described with the label "paralinguistic"). Second, it is generally acknowledged that, in any event, punctuation does not do a very good job of rendering spoken intonations. For example, Bolinger (1975) says: "In its miserly regard for intonation, print allows us only nine marks, and even then mixes logical considerations with intonational ones." And Sampson (1985) provides a demonstration of the "incompleteness" of English orthography by contrasting the ways in which four different intonational contours, which are not distinguishable in writing, can affect the meaning of a spoken utterance of the question.   Note that these two factors conspire to ensure that punctuation will not have to be dealt with in detail. The observation that punctuation is a poor device for rendering intonation might present a serious problem for the claim of the expressive equivalence of written and spoken language, if intonation itself were not regarded as a relatively marginal feature of the spoken language.

---

example, the fact that in German, unlike English, all finite subordinate clauses are set off by commas). But such differences are relatively minor when considered in the light of the extraordinary cross-linguistic regularity in the use of indicators, even with respect to the marking of most categories of lexical grammar (see below).

LIMITS OF THE TRANSCRIPTIONAL VIEW

That this "transcriptional" view of punctuation still has wide uncritical acceptance among linguists bears witness to the dominance of the contrastive approach to written language. Considered on its own terms, however, the picture is both empirically unwarranted and theoretically incoherent. Let me begin with the empirical problems. It is true that punctuation originated in part as a device for the transcription of intonation (or analogously, as an aid for recitation or performance), in an age when the acts of reading and transcription were generally accompanied by oral recitation of the text. But even in scribal traditions, it appears, the fit between punctuation and intonation was at best only approximate, and the two systems came to diverge increasingly over the course of development of print traditions.[7]

In a number of cases, to be sure, there is some correspondence between the use of punctuation marks and intonational boundaries of various sorts, notably as regards commas, periods and dashes (the only marks, I should note, that are ordinarily used in the transcription of spoken discourse). But even here the fit is only approximate. This is evident in consideration of various studies of the sorts of punctuation errors made by student writers, who tend to follow the model of intonation too slavishly in inserting punctuation. For example, novice writers often insert commas after syntactically complex or contrastively stressed subject noun phrases, as in

(2.1)   The constant change which Humpty Dumpty talks about, is neither practical nor responsible. [Cited in Chafe and Danielewicz (1985)]

(2.2)   Percy didn't approve of the idea, but his wife, was very keen. [Cited in Cruttenden (1986)]

In addition, commas are often inserted before various sentential complements, as in:

---

[7]See Levinson (1986) for a discussion of the use of punctuation in the English and Latin scribal traditions.

(2.3)   It is true, that it is not necessary to state this entire phrase.
         [Cited in Chafe and Danielewicz (1985)]

(Note that these patterns of punctuation were the norm in English
until the late eighteenth century, at a time when English punctuation
was more closely tied to intonation.) On the other hand, commas are
often required where no intonational break is present in speech, such
as before certain interpolations (as in *John, as I said, will not be here*),
which are often spoken as associated with the preceding element
under a single falling contour.

When we consider other punctuation marks, moreover, we find
that punctuational distinctions most often do not correlate reliably
with any intonational cues. Consider the examples in (2.4) and (2.5),
for example:

(2.4a)   Order your furniture on Monday, take it home on Tuesday.
(2.4b)   Order your furniture on Monday; take it home on Tuesday.
(2.5a)   He reported the decision: we were forbidden to speak with
         the chairman directly.
(2.5b)   He reported the decision; we were forbidden to speak with
         the chairman directly.
(2.5c)   He reported the decision – we were forbidden to speak with
         the chairman directly.

These pairs are quite clearly distinct in meaning. Example (2.4a) is
the sort of conditional one would expect to find in an advertisement:
"If you order it on Monday, you can take it home on Tuesday";
(2.4b), by contrast, is simply the conjunction of two commands: "do
X and do Y." In (2.5a), the second clause is interpreted as an
elaboration of what was decided; in (2.5b), as an explanation of why
the decision was reported as it was; and in (2.5c), the second clause
admits of either interpretation. But in informal experiments, I have
found that speakers are unable to signal these differences reliably to
other speakers.   (The existence of (2.5c) makes this point
persuasively; if there is a single intonation associated with this use of
the dash, then it would have to be neutral with respect to the two
interpretations. But in that case, we would expect that the same

intonation would be transcribable using either the colon or the semicolon.)

To be sure, examples like these often suggest intonational differences to the reader; many people report that they can imagine reading them aloud so as to convey the intended sense-distinctions. On the face of things, this observation is curious, inasmuch as marks like the semicolon and colon are virtually never used in transcription of ordinary spoken discourse: if there is in fact a characteristic intonation associated with these marks, where is it heard, and how is it learned? One possible answer is that the intonational correlates of marks like the semicolon, quotation mark or parenthesis do in fact exist in the specialized spoken genre used for reading aloud, which is used in what we might call the "transdiction" of written texts. Thus there may be some truth to Bolinger's (1975) observation that the parenthesis "signifies an overall drop in pitch, with the normal internal pitch contrasts still maintained at the lower level," at least in the sense that that prosodic feature is used to render the parenthetical when we encounter it in a text we are reading aloud. But rather than saying that the parenthesis "signifies a drop in pitch," we would do better to say that "a drop in pitch is used in certain registers to pronounce the parenthesis." And in the same way, experienced broadcasters often use a combination of pause and ironic tone to indicate the direct quotation in their reading of a sentence like *The new-wave publications are full of advertisements for business consultants offering "prosperity consciousness discovery groups," and for support groups for "recovering Catholics."* But it would clearly be odd to claim that written-language quotation marks – at least as used by educated writers – were "transcriptions" of a particular spoken-language intonation.

These observations suggest that there is grounds for doubting whether punctuation can be said to function as a device for "indicating" or "signifying" intonational features. But note in fact that standard formulations of the relation would be suspect even if the fit between punctuation and intonation were perfect. What would it mean to say that a comma "indicates" a certain intonational boundary, for example, when the text in which it is inscribed is never spoken? The statement could be interpreted as a claim about how most writers initially learn the use of commas, but it isn't clear what relevance that would have to the description of the rule that competent writers consult when using commas, nor is it necessary that every learner proceed in this way (congenitally deaf persons can learn to punctuate, after all). Or it could mean that hearing readers tend to associate a kind of internal "acoustic image" with the presence of certain punctuation marks. This claim is surely right, in some sense; I suspect that it is what linguists have in mind when they endorse the transcriptional view of punctuation, and what writers are getting at when they say, for example, that the knowledge of how to use the comma depends in the end on having "a good ear" or "a rhythmic sense." But whatever the psychological mechanism associated with such inner voices, it is not clear what explanatory purpose would be served by saying that punctuation "transcribes" them, particularly when, as with colons or parentheses, they have no actual correlates in ordinary speech.[8]

What the transcriptional view of punctuation buys us, in the end, is a theoretically uninteresting account of what is in any event a not very good correlation. To proceed with the analysis of punctuation, then, we will be best off setting aside the contrastive point of view, and approaching punctuation (and more) as an autonomous system that admits of study in its own terms. It may turn out that punctuation and intonation are sometimes used to convey the same kinds of information, just as the English passive and the Romance reflexive do; but that should not be a starting point for the analysis of either system.

---

[8]It is significant that there are conventions for reading aloud associated with all written languages, even Classical Chinese, in which the writing system is not alphabetic, and the written language has so many homonyms as to be virtually incomprehensible to a listener who does not have the written text before him (Sampson (1980)). This suggests that the availability of an acoustic image is highly important, if clearly not essential, to the process of reading. But whatever the psychological interest of these observations, they should not be allowed to intrude on the linguistic analysis of written language.

3 THE GRAMMAR OF TEXT-CATEGORIES

The term "punctuation" is generally used to refer to a category defined in partially graphic terms: a set of non-alphanumeric characters that are used to provide information about structural relations among elements of a text, including commas, semicolons, colons, periods, parentheses, quotation marks and so forth. From the point of view of function, however, punctuation must be considered together with a variety of other graphical features of the text, including font- and face-alternations, capitalization, indentation and spacing, all of which can be used to the same sorts of purposes. From here on, I will talk about all of these graphical devices as instances of *text-category indicators* of written language.

Graphically, indicators can mark off categories in one of three ways: by delimiting one or both ends of an element of a particular type, by separating two elements of the same type, or by typographically distinguishing an element of a particular type from its surroundings. Note however that category indicators can't be classified on the basis of their graphical properties alone, since the same graphical device may have multiple functions. Thus the period functions both as a text-sentence-delimiter and a marker of lexical abbreviations, and an initial capital letter serves both to delimit sentences and mark "proper expressions" (i.e., proper nouns and adjectives). Note also that the classification of a particular graphical device as a category indicator may depend on the particular written

17

genre that is under consideration. Thus a newline serves as a category indicator in lists (where it separates elements of the category "item"), and in poetry (where it separates elements of the category "line"). But the strings of characters separated by line breaks in running prose are not elements of any text category, which is to say that they are not domains that can figure in the definition of any syntactic or semantic rules for that genre.

The class of text-category indicators can be extended indefinitely to include a number of genre-specific devices used to mark off categories in running natural-language texts of various sorts, such as the section and chapter headings of a book, or the salutation of a letter. These in turn interact in various ways with a rich set of cross-indexing devices, such as footnotes and paragraph numbers, as well as with the various devices used in other ("non-running") text-genres such as diagrams, lists and tables. At present, however, there is no satisfactory scheme of classification for the range of graphical conventions used in the presentation of natural-language texts, so that it is difficult to say exactly how text-category indicators would fit into such a scheme, or in what ways they can be assimilated to the notational devices used in constructed languages of various types.[9]

For the present purposes, I will restrict myself to talking about those devices used to indicate categories at the level of the paragraph or below in ordinary written prose discourse. In particular, I will concentrate on those indicators which are "genre-independent": that is, which can be used in every written genre from a personal letter to a published article (thereby excluding, for example, footnotes, block quotations, bullet items, the newlines used in poetry and lists). The reason for restricting the discussion in this way is not just that these devices are the most widely used of category indicators, but also that they have a special status as "part of the written language." Thus we would say that knowing to use commas is part of "knowing how to write," whereas knowing how to use footnotes or headers is part of "knowing how to write a paper," or whatever.

---

[9]See Mountford (1980) and McCawley (ms), however, for some interesting remarks on various aspects of this problem.

One of the things I will be trying to show here is that this distinction has a theoretical basis. The text-category indicators we will be concerned with are part of a subsystem which is properly speaking "linguistic"; that is, which is constrained and organized along the same lines that appear to apply to other sorts of natural-language subsystems. It is this, more than anything else, that distinguishes these indicators from the other figural devices that are used in concert with natural-language in the construction of particular document genres (books, articles, machine interfaces, or whatever).

In order to make this point here, I will give an outline of some aspects of the syntactic, presentational (i.e., graphological) and semantic rules that determine the use of text-category indicators, contrasting them where relevant to analogous rules both of the spoken language and of other sorts of graphical systems and notational conventions.

Before proceeding, I should say something about method. I will be describing here the punctuational practices common among reputable contemporary American writers, with occasional remarks on other national styles. For the most part, I have confined myself to talking about rules of punctuation that a competent writer might be expected to know, as opposed to those for which authority is vested with specialists in the details of document preparation and production. (Thus a reputable author will probably have sound intuitions about when to use commas or parentheses to set off material, but is less likely to be familiar with the details of the rules for hyphenation of compounds, or with the rules for inserting spaces before or after ellipses.)

TWO GRAMMARS OF WRITTEN LANGUAGE

We will want to distinguish two different sorts of grammars (or if you prefer, two distinct levels of grammatical description) that are relevant to determining the distribution of explicit elements in the written language. The first of these I will call the "lexical grammar," that is, the grammar responsible to describe the dependencies that obtain among lexical items in the text. (This is the happiest term I can think of. I should note that I do not intend that it should be connected to any particular grammatical theory that happens to have the word "lexical" in its name.)

The written-language lexical grammar is the same sort of system that linguists generally call the "grammar," *tout court*, in talking about the spoken language, but there are certain differences to be kept in mind. First, as we noted, the lexical grammar of a particular written language may contain particular words and constructions that are not present in the spoken variety with which it is associated, and vice versa. More important, for our purposes, the lexical grammar of the written language may contain morphological, semantic, or syntactic categories that must be explicitly marked in writing, but which are not treated distinctively in speech. For example, there is nothing in the phonological representations of spoken-language words that requires the identification of a special class of abbreviations and contractions, such as are marked by the use of periods and apostrophes in the spelling of their written equivalents (though certain contractions may exhibit syntactic peculiarities in both varieties). By the same token, the written-language rules of hyphenation may require the explicit representation of distinctions that are not relevant to the statement of spoken-language rules of word formation, so as to capture the difference, say, between *middle-class students* and *students who are middle class*, or between *carefully planned party* and *well-planned party*. Finally, the written-language category of "proper expressions" (i.e., expressions marked by capitalization) quite obviously has no spoken-language equivalent. Note that this category cannot be identified on semantic or syntactic grounds alone; in English, it includes both common nouns (*Frenchman, Congressional Medal of Honor*) and adjectives (*Christlike, Hispanic*).

By contrast, I will use the term "text grammar" for the rules that describe the distribution of certain explicitly marked categories like the paragraph, (text-) sentence, and dash-interpolation, which classify the role that the content of lexical constituents relative to a certain structure of argument and context of interpretation. To a large extent, the well-formedness conditions imposed by the text-grammar can be stated in ways that are independent of the content of lexical categories, though the relationship between the two grammars is complicated, and will be best considered in terms of specific examples. In particular, we will see that certain kinds of written-language categories, such as the parenthetical, must be regarded as figuring as categories of both the lexical grammar and the text-grammar, and moreover that they are subject to different constraints and interpreted differently according to the level at which they are introduced. Observations about categories like these will prove to be important in distinguishing the two types of grammatical system.[10]

I should stress that I am using the term "text grammar" here in a relatively literal sense, in distinction to the way the term is used in much of the literature on discourse analysis. Thus the "text" is to be understood only as a passage of written language (and not simply as an extended stretch of discourse in any mode), and the term "grammar" is to be understood as a set of rules that determine syntactic relations among explicit formal elements (as opposed to describing essentially semantic or pragmatic relations of "coherence" and the like). Of course text-grammatical categories like the text-sentence and paragraph are associated with rules of semantic interpretation, but the text-grammar, as the term is used here, is responsible to assign such interpretations only insofar as they correspond to the presence of formally explicit categories.

We can get a rough idea of the basic difference between the two kinds of grammars by considering t he difference between the two kinds of elements that people commonly refer to as "sentences." Traditional grammars and handbooks define the sentence in any of three ways: either syntactically (as a group of words

---

[10]Thus a discourse analyst might want to assign two different grammatical representations to a sentence like *Some people found the book fatuous; John considered it a paramount example of post-modern criticism,* depending as the second clause is interpreted as an "exemplification" (assuming that John considers post-modern criticism fatuous) or as a "qualification" or "adversative" (on the assumption that John admires post-modernism). From our point of view, however, this is a distinction that corresponds to no demonstrable formal difference, and so will be ignored in assigning a structural representation to the sentence, though I will take up cases like these in the chapter on the semantics of text-categories.

"that contains a subject and a predicate"); or prosodically (as a group of words "that can be uttered by itself" or "that can be followed by a pause"); or semantically (as a group of words "that expresses a proposition" or "that conveys a statement, question, command or exclamation" or "that expresses a complete thought"). Each of these definitions is an attempt to come to grips with what we will call the "lexical sentence," the linguistic type that constitutes the object of inquiry of both traditional and modern grammatical analysis. But none of them deals with what we will call the "text-sentence," which is the fundamental unit of text-grammatical structure (and not incidentally, of instruction in writing). The text-sentence is that unit of written texts that is customarily presented as bracketed by a capital letter and a period (though those properties are not criterial). It may consist only of a single lexical sentence, or it may contain a number of lexical sentences in various text-grammatical roles:

(3.1)   Caesar wept.

(3.2)   The poor cried; Caesar wept.

(3.3)   The poor (we would now call them the disadvantaged) cried; Caesar wept—what else would you have had him do?

By the same token, the lexical content of a text-sentence need not be a lexical sentence in its own right, notwithstanding the fulminations of schoolroom grammarians:

(3.4)   The L9000 delivers everything you wanted in a luxury sedan. With more power. At a price you can afford.

(3.5)   This will solve the immediate housing problem. But at what cost?

In the discussion of semantics below, I will return to the fundamental question of how lexical sentences and text-sentences are related. For the present, it is enough to observe that the two types are clearly different sorts of linguistic objects, which figure in different grammatical systems.

SOME GENERAL PROPERTIES OF TEXT-GRAMMARS

In this monograph, I'll be interested in making several basic points about the grammar of categories like the text-sentence. First, this grammar is in important ways autonomous of the properties of the lexical grammar, which is to say that well-formedness conditions on text-grammatical structures can be stated without reference to the categories and conditions that determine the well-formedness of lexical structures. This point is not always apparent, inasmuch as standard texts and handbooks spend a disproportionate amount of time talking about the use of those indicators (in particular, commas) that are most sensitive to aspects of lexical structure.

Second, the text-grammar, like the lexical grammar, is largely a matter of tacit knowledge: as we will see, most of its more interesting properties are not accessible to casual reflection, and are not described in any of the standard handbooks. And finally, the text-grammar is essentially *linguistic*, which is to say that its rules are most naturally described by means of the same sorts of devices that linguists have brought to bear to describe syntactic and phonological regularities in the spoken language, and that they are interconstrained in a way that we have come to associate with linguistic subsystems.

4 The Syntax of Text-Categories

In this chapter and the next, I will outline various aspects of the syntax and presentation rules (that is, the graphology) of the text grammar. In the chapter following these, I will say something about the semantic rules associated with text-grammatical categories. Taken in its entirety, the text grammar is much too complex to permit anything like a complete description within the scope of this discussion. What I want to do, rather, is to discuss some of these rules and their interaction in sufficient detail to make the general point I am after: that the system of text categories makes use of the same sorts of formal devices that operate in other domains of natural language, and that its description is naturally regarded as a linguistic enterprise. For this reason, I won't be concerned in the course of this discussion with the question of which descriptive framework is most appropriate for text-grammatical description, and I will try to present my observations, where possible, in a theory-neutral way.

The basic units of text structure are the paragraph and the text-sentence, which correspond to the basic structural categories in the representation of the argument structure of the text interpretation. The syntax of the paragraph is quite simple, so long as we confine ourselves to straightforward exposition: a paragraph consists of one or more text-sentences. The immediate structure of the text-sentence is also relatively simple. A text sentence consists of a single text-clause, or of two or more text-clauses, which are ordinarily presented as separated by semicolons:

(4.1)   John took French.

(4.2)   John took French; Susan took Spanish.

(4.3)   John took French; Susan took Spanish; Annette took Russian.

and so forth.

It is at the level of text-clause structure that complications begin to set in. Each text-clause must minimally contain a head that is normatively, but by no means invariably, a well-formed lexical sentence. Thus we will assume that all of the elements separated by semicolons in each of the following examples will count as well-formed text-clauses:

(4.4)   Not me; I'm going home.

(4.5)   A quorum?; not on your life.

As a general matter, I will assume that the syntax of the text-grammar imposes no explicit conditions of well-formedness on the lexical content of its constituent clauses, though as we will see below, such conditions may be implicit in the rules of interpretation assigned to text-grammatical categories.

Now we come to the constituency of the text-clause itself. Note first that each text-clause can have only a single head, or to put this another way, that the category "text-clause" does not directly recurse as an expansion of itself. Thus a sequence of text-clauses separated by semicolons must be interpreted as conjoined at the same level:

(4.6)   The students were allowed to choose which language they wanted to study; Jan took Spanish.

(4.7)   Jan took Spanish; Betty took French.

(4.8)   *The students were allowed to choose which language they wanted to study; Jan took Spanish; Betty took French.

CLAUSAL ADJUNCTS: THE COLON-EXPANSION

The structure of clauses becomes more complex when we consider the category of clausal adjuncts, which includes what we can think of as colon-expansions, "dash-interpolations" (strings of words delimited by dashes) and parentheticals (a term I am using here in its literal sense, to refer to an element contained within parentheses).[11] Of these adjuncts, the colon-expansion is the most straightforward in its syntax. Several properties are particularly relevant here. First, the colon expansion is always the rightmost element of the text-clause that contains it, whatever the position of the lexical element that functions semantically as its "antecedent" (not a happy term, but the best available to denote the element of whose content it provides an expansion or elaboration):

(4.9)   He told the press his reason: he did not want have to renegotiate his contract; but he did not give any explanation to the team owners.

(4.10)   *He told the press his reason: he did not want have to renegotiate his contract, but he did not give any explanation to the team owners.

(4.11)   *His reason: he did not want have to renegotiate his contract (,) was clear to the fans.

In this respect, note that the colon-expansion behaves very much like the "extraposed" relative clause of sentences like:

(4.12)   Jackson gives several arguments in the last section that are particularly compelling.

(4.13)   There's a woman on line seven who says she has to speak with you.

Note, by the way, that both colon expansions and extraposed relative clauses can have multiple heads; cf. the similarities between (4.14) and (4.15):

(4.14)   We have a man on line seven and a woman on line two who want to talk about the A's winning streak.

---

[11]I exclude from discussion here certain specialized uses of parentheses, such as to set off dates within references and section- or example-numbers. Similarly, I exclude the use of dashes (technically, en dashes) to indicate inclusive dates or numbers, as in <1971–73>, and the use of 2- and 3-em dashes to indicate ellipsis or missing letters or to introduce dialogue.

(4.15)   Brown pointed out the costs to the community on the radio
last night, and Mitchell mentioned the political consequence
in this morning's paper: the bill will cost the taxpayers more
than $100,000 in the first year, and may be seen as giving the
Republicans an unfair electoral advantage.

Syntactically, then, we might describe the colon-expansion by
means of any of the devices used to handle extraposed relatives and
analogous constructions (though with provisos for the fact that
extraposition of colon-expansions is "obligatory" and that the colon-
expansion must be the rightmost element of its clause): by means of a
movement transformation, by means of some device that allowed for
discontinuous constituency, or by simply generating the colon-
expansion in place as a clausal constituent, and leaving to the
semantics the job of determining which element of the preceding
clause it is associated with.

For the present purposes, I will assume the third line of analysis.
For one thing, it avoids complications raised for the assignment of
constituency where multiple heads are involved, as in (4.14) and
(4.15). For another thing, it entails that the colon-expansion will itself
always be a text-clause constituent, and thereby simplifies the
statement of the restriction on the appearance of colon-expansions in
other than clause-final position, which can now be handled by means
of a straightforward phrase-structure rule, for example as:

$$C_t \rightarrow P_t^+ \ (E_c)$$

where C_t is a text clause, E_c is a colon-expansion, and P_t+ is a
sequence of one or more text-phrases (a category to be discussed
further below).[12]

---

[12]Note by the way that there are other graphical devices used in the
presentation of running text that seem to behave in an analogous way. In
most styles, for example, footnotes can appear only at the end of a text-
sentence, even if the material that is elaborated or explained in the note is
contained earlier in the sentence. Thus we would write:

(i)   Several other writers have mentioned this construction, though
Jones is the only one to treat it in detail.[1]
[1]See, e.g., Smith (1985), Bernstein (1986).

THE CONTENT OF COLON-EXPANSIONS

As with other text-categories, I will assume here that the text-grammar imposes no constraints on the lexical content of colon-expansions. In this connection, note that the antecedent of a colon-expansion is often, but not invariably, a noun-phrase; we also find colon-expansions whose heads are prepositional phrases, as in (4.16), verb phrases, as in (4.17), and entire sentences, as in (4.18) and (4.19):

(4.16) The ship steered between the buoy and the island: the only course that would avoid the rocky shoals.

(4.17) She grabbed her attacker by the thumb: the ideal action for getting him to release his grip.

(4.18) He called the hotel: no answer.

(4.19) I will be frank: there is no way you're going to get the job.

Thus the footnote in this example can be regarded as "extraposed" from the material it indexes. In this case, however, the explanation for the regularity is relatively obvious: it would place an excessive demand on the reader to ask him to interrupt his reading of the sentence to refer to a note at another point in the text, and then return to complete the sentence. In the case of the colon-expansion, however, such a line of explanation is not available, since the material in the expansion could generally be presented at a point adjacent to the antecedent of the expansion by means of another text-category, such as the dash-interpolation, with a roughly equivalent semantic force:

(*ii*)   His real objection – the contract made no provision for sick leave – was easy enough to perceive.

(*iii*) His real objection was easy enough to perceive: the contract made no provision for sick leave.

It is arguable that (*ii*) and (*iii*) are subtly distinct in meaning, but it would be difficult to maintain that the difference is such as would make (*iii*) impossible to parse if the colon-expansion immediately followed the antecedent his real objection. Here as with other aspects of text-grammar, it is hard to argue that all of the constraints on the system could be derived from the application of general principles of rational organization.

By the same token, we note that a colon-expansion can itself consist of any element from a sequence of one or more text-clauses down to a single noun phrase:

(4.20)   He told us his preference: Jan would take Spanish; Betty would take French.

(4.21)   The research committee will have only one responsibility: to prepare the year-end reports.

(4.22)   He told us his preference: strawberries.

The only constraints on the content of the colon-expansions, then, appear to be semantic: can the lexical content be plausibly interpreted as an elaboration or expansion of some element in the preceding lexical clause?[13] (Of course, this notion of "elaboration" must be cashed in explicitly in the description of the interpretive rules associated with colon-expansion.) We will assume, then, that the text-grammar merely makes provision for the rewriting of the colon-expansion as a sequence of one or more text-clauses (allowing, as we noted earlier, that rule expanding the text-clause itself imposes no constraints on its lexical content):[14]

---

[13]To be sure, the form of a colon expansion is also subject to what appear to be morphological constraints. For example an E_c cannot consist of a (verbal) passive VP, as in:

(i)   *He told us what he would be: elected by a great majority/awarded the Nobel Prize/ very tired of his job etc.

But this constraint here is an instance of a more general constraint on the distribution of passive VP's, which is relevant as well in purely lexical constructions in which text categories do not figure at all, such as in (ii):

(ii)   *What he would soon be was elected by a great majority/ awarded the Nobel Prize

Thus this constraint is best explained as a consequence of the rules of interpretation associated with passive VP's, rather than as a constraint particular to the text grammar.

[14]Note, by the way, that some writers allow a colon-expansion to consist of one or more text-sentences or paragraphs:

(i)   There are several things we have to do before the conference starts: Bette has to prepare the brochures. Someone should make sure the registration tables have been ordered from Facilities.

$$E_C \rightarrow C_t{}^+$$

There is, however, one further constraint on the content of the colon-expansion that should be mentioned. Note that a colon-expansion cannot itself contain a colon-expansion at any level of embedding (so that we might say that the rule introducing colon-expansions is non-recursive). Thus (4.23) and (4.24) are ungrammatical, despite the fact that they have obvious interpretations:

(4.23)   *They serve a lot of cajun dishes: blackened redfish, gumbo, and one thing you don't see a lot of: catfish sushi.

(4.24)   *Management has instituted a new policy: the research budget will be set by the lab managers; the old research committee will have only one responsibility: to prepare the year-end reports.

Note, moreover, that (4.25) is ambiguous, depending on whether the second text-clause after the colon is interpreted as being part of the expansion, whereas (4.26) allows only one grammatical reading:

(4.25)   The press secretary gave them the rules: they were not allowed to speak to the committee directly; all other members were forbidden to discuss what the committee had decided.

(4.26)   The press secretary gave them the rules: they were not allowed to speak to the committee directly; all other members were forbidden to discuss what the committee had decided: a hiring freeze would take place.

(*ii*)   We propose a three-part program designed to address these problems: ¶ First, a committee will be formed with the task of deciding on a policy for new equipment acquisitions. . . .

It is not clear whether the content of the expansions in (*i*) and (*ii*) should be considered part of the embedding clauses, or whether the colon in these cases represents a kind of sentence-final punctuation. Perhaps for just this reason, many writers (myself among them) are leery of this construction, unless the material in the colon-expansion is a quotation an example sentence, or a (graphically explicit) list.

I will discuss this restriction further in the following chapter, where we will see that it is an instance of a more general constraint on the embedding of text-adjuncts of all types.

OTHER ADJUNCTS: THE PARENTHETICAL AND THE DASH-INTERPOLATION

The dash-interpolation and the parenthetical differ from the colon-expansion in several respects. The parenthetical can occur as a constituent of any text-category from the text itself (in which case it may contain one or more paragraphs) down to the word (in which case it may contain an affix or a single character). The dash-interpolation occurs only at the level of the text-clause. Unlike the colon-expansion, these categories need not be the rightmost constituents of the text-clause in which they occur:

(4.27)   He then sailed around the Horn (the voyage was eventful) and returned to Madras in April.

(4.28)   He then sailed around the Horn – the voyage was eventful – and returned to Madras in April.

Nonetheless, the three categories have a sufficient number of syntactic properties in common to warrant their classification as instances of a single text-syntactic category, the adjunct. First, we note that, like colon-expansions, neither a parenthetical nor a dash-interpolation can appear in initial position of a text-category that dominates it. This is clear in the case of parentheticals, as shown by (4.29)–(4.34):

(4.29)   *¶(The majority of the ships are flying Panamanian flags.) The government has not yet announced whether it will retaliate for the mining. . .

(4.30)   *(Not surprisingly), she left.

(4.31)   And (not surprisingly), she left.

(4.32)   *He stayed; (not surprisingly), she left.

(4.33)   *He told us the news: (not surprisingly), she left.

(4.34)   *When the announcement came – (not surprisingly) she left – they took it well.

In the case of the dash-interpolation, this point may be a bit less obvious, inasmuch as the presentation rules for punctuation marks would not in any case allow the dash to appear in sentence- or clause-initial position (see the following chapter). Nonetheless, the restriction should be clear enough in the following examples:

(4.35)   And – what's more surprising – she left.

(4.36)   He stayed. *What's more surprising – she left.

(4.37)   *He stayed; what's more surprising – she left.

For the moment, let us say that the difference between colon-expansions and the other adjuncts is explained by supposing that the categories that dominate parentheticals and dash-interpolations are what we will call *text-phrases* (F_t), and that such phrases are introduced by rules of the form:

$$C_t \rightarrow F_t^+$$

$$F_t \rightarrow E\,(A)$$

where F_t is a text-phrase, and E is simply a lexical expression whose form is unconstrained by the text-grammar. Note that the assumption of a rule of this form will also explain why we do not find sequences of a dash-interpolation followed by a parenthetical, as in:

(4.41)   *She walked out – who could blame her – (it was during the chainsaw scene, as I recall) and went directly home.

As an adjunct, the parenthetical in (4.38) could not be generated either in the final position of the preceding text-phrase (since the rule we have formulated provides for only one adjunct per phrase), nor in initial position in the text-phrase that dominates it. Note also that this formulation allows us to generalize the rule we gave earlier that provided for the expansion of a text-clause as a text-phrase followed by a colon-expansion. We will assume instead a general rule that provides for the expansion of any text-category as a head and an adjunct of the relevant level; the colon-expansion, but not the dash-interpolation or the parenthetical, will be subcategorized as a category that occurs only at the clausal level.

There is an interesting class of apparent counter-examples to this line of analysis. Note that, in contradistinction to sentences like (4.41), we do find sequences of a parenthetical followed by a dash-interpolation, as in:

(4.42)   We saw the movie (which had been banned in Boston) – Jane insisted on going – but we were unimpressed.

But we can explain the occurrence of sentences like (4.42) by saying that the parenthetical there is really a constituent of a lexical phase, rather than of a (graphically identical) text-phrase, so that the dash-interpolation in (4.42) is not really text-category-initial. I have already mentioned the need for allowing parentheticals to be generated as elements of lexical phrases, and will return to this matter below. For the moment, however, note that there is support for this analysis in the observation that the only parentheticals that can appear in sentences like this are those "parentheticals of elaboration" whose content could be generated by the lexical phrase-structure rules that would normally operate on their lexical heads (in this case, to produce the relative clause *which had been banned in Boston*). Thus we cannot get a sentence like:

(4.43)   *We saw the movie (it had been banned in Boston; they'll ban anything for a price) – a three-hour film, I might add – but we were unimpressed.

where the parenthetical could not be interpreted as providing an alternative expansion of the preceding NP, but must instead be assumed to be a text-level adjunct, which like the colon-expansion can be rewritten as a sequence of one or more text-clauses. Thus we see that the same element (in the case of (4.43), the phrase *We saw the movie*) can be regarded as either a lexical or text-phrase for purposes of assignment of a parenthetical adjunct. The possibility of this sort of dual analysis will be relevant in a somewhat different way when we come to talk about the uses of the comma.[15]

---

[15]There is further evidence for the analysis of parentheticals as falling into two classes in the observation that a parenthetical cannot precede a dash-interpolation when it is not adjacent to its antecedent:

In this connection, note that the dash-interpolation, as well, can be rewritten as a sequence of text-clauses, as in:

(4.44)   The ship was poorly provisioned – the biscuits were maggoty; the rum was watered down – and many of the sailors became ill.

Thus we have another reason for grouping dash-interpolations and (text-level) parentheticals together with colon-expansions under a single category of adjuncts, which are subject to a single rewrite rule:

$$A_t \rightarrow C_t{}^+$$

(That is, a text-adjunct expands as a sequence of one or more text clauses.)

Finally, note that like the colon-expansion, neither the dash-interpolation nor the parenthetical can contain an adjunct of the same type, though adjuncts of other types are acceptable:

(4.45)   *Jones (an employee (actually, a director) of the firm) was also present.

(4.46)   Jones (an employee – actually, a director – of the firm) was also present.

(4.47)   *Holding the bat firmly – her father – himself a former major leaguer – had given it to her– she awaited the pitch.

(4.48)   Holding the bat firmly – her father (himself a former major leaguer) had given it to her – she awaited the pitch.

(i)   *An employee entered (actually, the bank director) – the door was open – and announced that the meeting was beginning.

The assumption here must be that the assignment of antecedent of the parenthetical in (i), like that of a colon-expansion, is determined by the same kinds of rules that determine the antecedent of a colon-expansion; note that the relation between the phrase *the bank director* and *an employee* would not be fixed by any lexical rules of coreference. Therefore the parenthetical here is appropriately treated as a text-adjunct, and so the dash interpolation is text-category-initial, and so the sentence is ungrammatical.

Thus if we treat adjuncts as a single class, we can use whatever mechanism is used to block the self-embedding of colon-expansions to block the self-embedding of text-adjuncts in general; we will say that a text-adjunct of any type A does not embed in a text-adjunct of the same type. This restriction could be expressed by means of any of several familiar mechanisms.[16]

THE INTERACTION OF TEXT-GRAMMAR AND LEXICAL GRAMMAR: COMMAS

I will return to the discussion of text-category adjuncts below, particularly as regards the proper treatment of parentheticals. For the moment, however, we can turn our attention to the interaction of the text grammar with the lexical grammar of the written language. I said earlier that I would not be discussing those indicators that are used to mark only categories of the lexical grammar, but we have seen that in one case, the parenthetical, we must be prepared to recognize that a single type of category can occur as an element of both the text-grammar and lexical grammar of the written language. The other indicator that plays a major role in both levels of description is the comma, but here the situation is somewhat different.

Standard handbooks list some ten or twenty uses of the comma, but for our purposes, we need recognize only two main classes. First, there is the class of elements *delimited* by commas, either at both ends (when the elements occur clause-internally) or at one end (roughly, when the elements are either clause-initial or -final).

The delimiter comma is contrasted with what we will call the *separator comma*, which is inserted between members of certain types

---

[16]For example, we could suppose that there exists a feature-passing convention which ensures that the features on the node of any adjunct are passed to all its children. We then further assume that the rule introducing adjuncts requires that an adjunct cannot be introduced as an expansion of a category that is already marked with a feature of the same type: thus a parenthetical could not be introduced as a constituent of a text-phrase or text-clause that is already marked with the feature [+paren]. But there are other ways to accomplish this, of course, and I have no brief to make for this particular treatment.

of conjoined elements, sometimes without an explicit conjunction, and sometimes with one. The obvious reason for distinguishing these two types of commas is that they involve different sorts of presentation rules: one comma goes *around* an element of a particular type, whereas the other goes *between* elements of the same type.[17] More explicitly, delimiter commas are introduced by a rule that makes reference to a single element of a certain category type, which is presented as delimited by commas (subject to various presentation rules of adjustment and "absorption," to be discussed below, which ensure, for example, that a comma is not presented at a clause- or sentence-boundary). The rule that introduces separator commas, on the other hand, must make reference to the regular expression instantiated by the elements of a conjunction. (I will have more to say about the form of these rules in the following chapter.) But there are also significant grammatical correlates to the distinction between the two types of commas, and I will try to show how these differences warrant their treatment as elements of separate grammatical systems.

The class of comma-delimited elements includes a variety of grammatical categories, among them various adverbial expressions, nonrestrictive relative clauses and appositives, vocatives, certain

---

[17]There is probably a third type of comma, which cannot be obviously assimilated to either of these others. This comma separates elements of different syntactic types. Sometimes it is used to avoid a parsing difficulty or an ambiguity, as in:

(*i*) Those students who can, contribute to the United Fund.

(*ii*) Such women as you, are seldom troubled with remorse.

The first example is the usage recommended by a standard freshman rhetoric; the second is cited by Fowler (1926), who goes on to say, however: "This device is illegitimate. Such sentences should be recast. . ."

A more clearly acceptable case involves the use of the comma to indicate omitted material, as in gapped sentences like:

(*iii*) Some people regard these problems as serious; others, as trivial.

I will not discuss these uses here, nor will I talk about the use of the comma in dates, bibliographic references, or other specialized formulae.

right-node-raised elements, and "parentheticals" in the broad sense –
i.e., interpolated expressions like "I hear" and "to be blunt":[18]

(4.49)   The key, *obviously*, has been lost.

(4.50)   The key, *which I did not have duplicated*, has been lost.

(4.51)   The key, *Mother*, has been lost.

(4.52)   The key, *if John is to be believed*, has been lost.

(4.53)   I saw, *as John opened the storeroom*, that the treasure had been plundered.

(4.54)   Jane lost, *and Bill found*, the key to the storeroom.

In our discussion of presentation rules below, we will see that all of
these categories are presented by a general rule that brackets
expressions of a certain type with commas; other presentation rules
will determine whether such commas are actually presented in the
text string. Thus delimiter commas are also involved in sentences
like (4.55)–(4.59), even though only one comma is presented in each
case:[19]

(4.55)   *Obviously*, the key has been lost.

(4.56)   The key has been lost, *obviously*.

(4.57)   The key has been lost, *obviously*; we can't get in.

(4.58)   We can't get in; *obviously*, the key has been lost.

(4.59)   The key, *obviously* – or at least, *apparently* – has been lost.

It is obviously not possible here to provide an analysis of the
syntax and semantics of each of these constructions, much less to try

---

[18]I would argue that this class also includes various prepositional
phrases, as in Fowler's example *The master beat the pupil, with a stick*, and
more interestingly, such conjoined VP's as are introduced with commas, as
in *Every president since then has either died, or become ill* and *He drank, and
drank as if there were no tomorrow*. The analysis of these last examples is
particularly interesting, but would take us too far afield.

[19]Meyer (1983) makes a similar suggestion along these lines for treatment
of initial and final delimiter commas. As we will see in the following
chapter, this observation can be integrated into a much more comprehensive
set of rules for the presentation of text-category indicators.

to characterize them in such a way as to say what they have in common. In a rough way, however, we observe that they all involve constituency problems, so that they do not behave as constituents, for example, under such tests as verb-phrase ellipsis.[20] What is more, all of them can be characterized as supplying material that is communicatively supererogatory to the bare propositional content of the lexical clause in which they appear. In this connection, note that traditional explanations of the use of the comma often try to classify all of these cases in terms of characterizations like "elements that do not change the meaning of the sentence." That is surely badly put, but the intuition behind it should be respected. Suppose we were going to construct a representation of the argument structure of a passage that looked something like an annotated proof. Then we would treat the content of most of these comma-delimited elements differently from the content of the rest of the sentence in which they appear, as something to be listed in the column reserved for annotations. (Thus we would write "the key is lost" as an axiom or claim, and put down "apparently" as a rule of inference or justification for the claim.) This is all very rough, but it does suggest that the content of these comma-delimited elements plays a distinctive role in the representation of the argument structure of the text.

The delimiter comma is contrasted with what we will call the *separator comma*, which is inserted between members of certain types of conjoined elements, sometimes without an explicit conjunction, and sometimes with one. These are the commas used with items in series, with conjoined sentences, and with conjoined adjectives, as in:

(4.60)   We put all our eggs in one basket, but we didn't keep our eye on it.

(4.61)   The woods are lovely, dark and deep.

(4.62)   It has a powerful, twenty-four valve engine.

(4.63)   Some players make millions, others make nothing.

---

[20]For discussion, see, e.g., McCawley (1982).

Here again, I will not try to provide an analysis of these constructions, beyond offering the observation that these cases quite clearly involve conjunction of terms, predicates or atomic propositions, in contrast to the comma-delimited elements I mentioned earlier.

PARENTHETICALS AND COMMAS

But there are independent reasons for considering these two uses of the comma as involving distinct linguistic types, which moreover figure at different levels of grammatical description. The first of these involves the distribution of parentheticals. Recall that we observed that the parenthetical, like other text-adjuncts, does not occur in the initial position of text-categories like the paragraph, text-sentence, or text-clause:

(4.64)   *¶(The majority of the ships are flying Panamanian flags.) The government has not yet announced whether it will retaliate for the mining. . .

(4.65)   *(Not surprisingly), she left.

(4.66)   *He stayed; (not surprisingly), she left.

(4.67)   *He told us the news: (not surprisingly), she left.

Now note that the parenthetical, alone among text-adjuncts, can occur as well as a constituent of lexical phrases, and that in such uses it can precede its head:

(4.68)   We expect (at least the majority of) the students to pass.

(4.69)   He presents a (pseudo-) formal analysis of the construction.

(4.70)   Every period of Christian history has produced (often bizarre) explanations of the book.

(4.71)   This view was unacceptable to (logical) positivists like Carnap.

(4.72)   This set, then, will be (properly) included in the set of integers.

(4.73)   He made his remarks to (then Secretary of State) Henry Kissinger.

Note that all of these examples involve the "parentheticals of elaboration" that I mentioned earlier, where the content of the parenthetical would be generated by an alternative application of the phrase-structure rules that generate its lexical head. (As we also observed, there is reason for treating these parentheticals as constituents of lexical phrases, rather than of text-phrases.) We observe that other types of parentheticals are not acceptable when they precede their heads:

(4.74) *They include (as they put it) "free gifts" with every purchase.

(4.75) They include "free gifts" (as they put it) with every purchase.

(4.76) *This set, then, will be (if I can use a technical term) subsected by the other one.

(4.77) This set, then, will be subsected (if I can use a technical term) by the other one.

(Sentences (4.74) and (4.76) do have unlikely readings in which the parenthetical is associated with a preceding term.)

But now note that lexical phrases containing initial parentheticals cannot appear in the initial position of comma-delimited elements, despite the fact that such examples appear to have straightforward interpretations:

(4.78) *The bombings, (then Secretary of State) Henry Kissinger announced, were an important step towards peace.

(4.79) *These films, (often bizarre) interpretations of the original book, have done well at the box office.

(4.80) *Carnap, (logical) positivist that he was, rejected this view.

This restriction in fact applies to other text-categories, such as the text-sentence and the text-clause:

(4.81) *(Logical) positivist that he was, Carnap rejected this view of meaning.

(4.82) *This view of meaning was popular at the period; (logical) positivists like Carnap, however, rejected it.

(4.83)   *This view was widely argued by the philosophers of the age
– (logical) positivists like Carnap excepted – but now has few
adherents.

(4.84)   *(Then Secretary of State) Henry Kissinger did not comment
on the move.

(4.85)   *Most administration officials supported the President in his
decision; (then Secretary of State) Henry Kissinger did not
comment on it.

By contrast, note that such parentheticals can appear after separator
commas, as in:

(4.86)   Among those present were Le Duc Tho, (then Secretary of
State) Henry Kissinger, and the French foreign minister.

(4.87)   The book mixes pointless anecdotes, (often bizarre)
interpretations of scripture, and rambling disquisitions on
the "new morality."

(4.88)   But proponents of this new, (logical) positivist view could
not countenance the introduction of such entities.[21]

How shall we account for these observations? Clearly there is no
problem with phrases like (*at least some of*) *his teachers* or (*logical*)
positivist themselves, which can occur freely in other positions.
Rather, we must suppose that there is a restriction that blocks the
appearance of initial parentheticals in the comma-delimited elements
in (4.78)–(4.80), but that no such restriction operates for the comma-
separated elements of examples (4.85)–(4.88). And inasmuch as this
same restriction applies to other text categories, such as the text-
sentence and the text-clause, we are led to conclude that the comma-
delimited categories of the lexical grammar must figure as categories
of the text-grammar as well. (Indeed, it is hard to see on what basis

---

[21]Note, by the way, that (4.87)-(4.89) are counterexamples to a categorical
rule often stated in handbooks to the effect that a parenthetical cannot be
preceded by a comma. The sentences presented to exemplify this dictum
always involve delimiter commas, as in *After the rain started, (around six
o'clock) we left the picnic.*

writers would be able to judge the ungrammaticality of (4.78)–(4.80), if not by analogy to other text-grammatical types.)

This suggests the need for an additional constraint on the appearance of adjuncts. The phrase-structure rule that introduces text-adjuncts only in the rightmost position of text-categories will not explain the non-occurrence of lexical parentheticals (i.e., parentheticals of elaboration) in the initial position of the comma-delimited elements in (4.78)–(4.80), or for that matter, in the initial position of other text-categories like the sentence, text-clause or dash-interpolation. As we have seen, such parentheticals would normally be generated in phrase-initial position by

rules that are independent of the text-grammar rule that introduces adjuncts. Instead, we must assume that the non-occurrence of parentheticals in text-category-initial position is due to a general constraint that blocks the appearance of parentheticals of all types in this position.[22]

By the same token, the fact that parentheticals can appear in the initial position of elements preceded by separator commas is evidence for assuming that these elements are not text-grammatical categories; these commas are relevant only to the lexical parsing of the text. The distinction is intuitively plausible, in the light of the observations we made about the functional role of the two sorts of elements. We expect the text-grammar to recognize those categories and distinctions that are relevant to the form of the argument structure of the text, as opposed to those categories that are relevant only to the determination of the propositional content of the argument constituents.

---

[22]It can be argued that such a constraint can be generalized to all adjuncts, and that it can further be invoked to explain why text-adjuncts – that is, text-parentheticals, dash interpolations and colon-expansions – occur only in the *rightmost* position of the clauses or phrases that contain them, whereas lexical parentheticals can appear anywhere *but* in initial position. In that case, we can assume that the work of getting adjunct order right is taken care of entirely by this constraint, and so that the phrase-structure rule that introduces text-adjuncts should be regarded as assigning only relations of immediate dominance.

Thus we will assume that comma-delimited elements (or as I will call them from here on, "lexical adjuncts") play a dual role: they figure as categories in both the text-grammar and the lexical grammar. By way of analogy, we can consider the role of the word, which figures as a category of both syntactic and morphological description. But as with the word, the two levels of analysis regard the relevant elements in quite different ways. We can assume, for example, that the text-grammar imposes no conditions on the lexical structure of an appositive clause (just as the lexical syntax is unconcerned with the derivational structure of the word). Rather, the text-grammar recognizes lexical phrases only to the extent that they figure differently in the construction of a representation of the argument structure of the text. This, in fact, will be the basis for the identification of the category of "text phrases" that we introduced earlier to serve as the heads of text-adjuncts like the (text-) parenthetical and the dash-interpolation.

"PROMOTION RULES": THE FORMAL DIFFERENCES BETWEEN
TEXT-GRAMMAR AND LEXICAL GRAMMAR

We can find further evidence to motivate this distinction in considering another difference between the two types of commas, this involving the infamous rule of "promotion to semicolon," which requires that when items containing commas are conjoined, all elements at the highest level shall be separated by semicolons, in place of the usual commas. Note that this rule applies only to separator commas:

(4.89)   Among the speakers were John; Ed; Rachel, a linguist; and Shirley.

(4.90)   Rachel will chair the first session, and the second session will be postponed; or I will chair both sessions.

(4.91)   *These decisions; which were ratified, or at least approved, by the full committee; were announced only last Wednesday.

(4.92)   *The speaker, John Wilson; who, apparently, wrote a book about Tinker, Evans and Chance; did not answer the question.

(4.93)   *In aping Christian observances, like other Victorian systems, including Positivism; it provided a rehabilitation school for honest doubters.

Note that this rule does not apply when only the last item in a series containing an explicit conjunction contains a comma, though it does apply when no explicit conjunction is present:[23]

(4.94)   Among the speakers will be John, Ed, and Rachel, a linguist.

(4.95)   The wagon was laden with an odd assortment of goods: pieces of furniture; piles of old rags; picture frames, a commodity that was evidently in much demand among the settlers.

Note also that the promotion rule applies only to the highest-level separators:

(4.96)   He has written books on Tinker, the shortstop; Evans, the second baseman; and Chance.

(4.97)   He has written books on Babe Ruth; on Tinker, the shortstop, Evans, the second baseman, and Chance; and on Hank Aaron.

(4.98)   *He has written books on Babe Ruth; on Tinker, the shortstop; Evans, the second baseman; and Chance; and on Hank Aaron.

(4.99)   Rachel will chair the first session, and the second session will be postponed, or I will chair both sessions; but you must inform the panelists before tomorrow.

---

[23]Note, by the way, that while the comma before *and* can be omitted in (*i*), the semicolon is obligatory in (*ii*). Depending on how the rule governing these alternations is formulated, this might be taken as evidence that the optional comma in (*i*) is in fact present at some level of representation.]

(*i*)   Rachel will chair the first session(,)and John will chair the second.

(*ii*)   Rachel will chair the first session, or there will be no chair; and John will chair the second.

(4.100)   *Rachel will chair the first session, and the second session will be postponed; or I will chair both sessions; but you must inform the panelists before tomorrow.

I do not want to get involved here in a detailed analysis of the promotion rule, or to suggest how it might best be formulated. For our purposes, it is enough to observe that it involves a complex dependency among the elements of a conjunction, so as to ensure, for example, that the first element of a series will be separated from the second by a semicolon if any term in the series (or any but the last term, if the series contains an explicit conjunction) contains a comma at any level of structure, and if the series is not itself dominated by a term belonging to another series or conjunction. It is an open question whether there are other rules in natural-language lexical syntax that demonstrate dependencies of this order of complexity, though certainly the formal apparatus exists with which such a rule can be stated. But it is important to note that there are no rules of remotely this order of complexity in the grammar of text-categories, which is far more highly constrained.

By way of example, we may consider the text-grammar rule of quote alternation, which treats a similar phenomenon in a quite different way. In American practice, this rule requires that double quotes be used for all top-level quotations, and that single quotes shall alternate with double quotes at successive levels of embedding:

(4.101)   Then the Lord said unto Moses: "Go in unto Pharoah, and tell him: 'Thus saith the Lord, the God of the Hebrews: "Let my people go, that they may serve me."'"[24]

---

[24]In British practice, of course, the order of quotes is reversed (and the placing of the final stop is different, though the rules for sequencing stops and quotations in traditional British practice are more complicated than most Americans suspect):

(i)   Then the Lord said unto Moses: 'Go in unto Pharoah, and tell him: "Thus saith the Lord, the God of the Hebrews: 'Let my people go, that they may serve me'"'.

I will discuss some of these details of presentation in the next chapter; they do not affect the argument I am making here.

Note that this alternation could be handled by a straightforward left-right parsing of the text, or by any formally equivalent device. One could imagine a "Twin-Earth" quote alternation rule, of course, that took a very different form; say where the unmarked form of the quote would be used in the most deeply embedded quotation, and where the alternation would proceed from there. This would give us, for example:

(4.102) Harry said, "Nobody goes there anymore."

(4.103) Harry said, 'Beth said, "Nobody goes there anymore."'

(4.104) Harry said, "It says here, 'Beth said, "Nobody goes there anymore."'"

and so on (though of course in Twin-Earth Britain they would do it the other way 'round).

But I am aware of no language that has such a rule of quote alternation, and it seems to me highly unlikely that any language should adopt such a rule for written natural-language texts. By contrast, note that the analogue of such a rule would be the natural bracketing convention to employ in a constructed language in which exactly two kinds of delimiters were used. One would write, for example:

$$a + (b * c)$$
$$a + [b * (c - d)]$$
$$a + (b * [c - (d * e)])$$

and so on. Note, moreover, that even our hypothetical rule of quote alternation is far simpler than the rule of comma-promotion, inasmuch as the choice of the outermost delimiter is determined entirely by the contents of the expression that it delimits; no reference need be made to the contents of the sisters of that expression.

If comma-delimited text-adjuncts are in fact text-categories, it would make sense that the rule of comma-promotion should not apply to them. It is clear that the rules that govern the distribution of text-category delimiters are more highly constrained than those that operate in lexical grammar, and that text-structure can be recovered by a more simple, left-to-right parsing mechanism than is required for lexical interpretation.[25] By contrast, the rule of comma-promotion requires a far more complex parser (arguably, in fact, one more complex than anything that is required for spoken-language syntax). Such a rule, in short, could not apply to text-category indicators, a claim for which there is in fact some interesting empirical evidence.[26]

---

[25]This is evident in consideration not only of the rule of quote alternation, but also of the distinction between lexical parentheticals, which can precede their heads, and text-parentheticals, which necessarily follow them.

[26]The evidence is complicated, and in some ways confounded, but it makes for an interesting tale. Note that Fowler (1926) recommended the practice of promoting both separator and delimiter commas (though he did not distinguish the two categories in those terms, of course). By way of example, he gave:

(*i*)   When ambition asserts the monstrous doctrine of millions made for individuals, their playthings, to be demolished at their caprice; is not the good man indignant?

Fowler further recommended the further promotion of semicolons to colons when the clauses separated contained internal semicolons:

(*ii*)   When ambition asserts the monstrous doctrine of millions made for individuals, their playthings, to be demolished at their caprice; sporting wantonly with the rights, the peace, the comforts, the existence, of nations, as if their intoxicated pride would, if possible, make God's earth their football: is not the good man indignant?

Note, however, that Fowler himself was inconsistent in his practice regarding these rules. The very sentence in which Fowler explains these examples reads:

(*iii*)   The previous semicolon, still having the same supreme task to do, and challenged by an upstart rival, has nothing for it but to change the regal for the imperial crown, and become a colon.(p 232)

Had Fowler adhered to his own rules, he would more likely have written either:

(*iv*)   The previous semicolon, still having the same supreme task to do, and challenged by an upstart rival; has nothing for it but to change the regal for the imperial crown, and become a colon.

or possibly even:

(*v*)   The previous semicolon; still having the same supreme task to do, and challenged by an upstart rival; has nothing for it but to change the regal for the imperial crown, and become a colon.

Seen abstractly, then, the syntax of text-categories can be regarded as a system that makes use of a somewhat constrained subset of natural-language structural devices, but whose structure nonetheless clearly reflects the organizational principles of spoken natural language. In the next chapter, I will examine some of the presentation rules for text-category indicators. These are rather more different from the rules of natural-language phonology than the corresponding rules of syntax, as one might expect on the basis of the fundamental differences between the nature of the different media for writing and speech. Nonetheless, we will see that here, too, the underlying principles of organization are reminiscent of the

---

And in the pages immediately following, we encounter a number of further examples in which Fowler violates his own recommendations (I leave the emendation of these examples as an exercise for the reader):

(*v i*)   They are to be regarded as devices, not for saving him the trouble of putting his words into the order that naturally gives the required meaning, but for saving his reader the moment or two that would sometimes, without them, be necessarily spent on reading the sentence two times over, once to catch the general arrangement, and again for the details. (p. 234)

(*v i i*)   The comma, most important, if slightest, of all stops, cannot indeed be got rid of, though even for that the full stop is substituted when possible; but the semicolon is now as much avoided by many writers as the colon (in its old use) by most. (p. 235)

(*v i i i*)   To group rightly then, we must take care, quite reversing the author's punctuation, that the first and second are separated by a stop of less power than that which separates the third from them. (p. 238)

(*i x*)   We need now only add two or three short specimens, worse, though from their shortness less remarkable, than the *Times* extract. (p. 239)

But Fowler could scarcely be accused of sloppiness; and in fact he never neglected the promotion rule where items in series and conjunctions are involved. In this case, rather, he was misled by his failure to recognize the distinction between separator and delimiter commas, and thus cast his recommendation more widely than the natural practice of even the most careful writer could have sustained.

presentation rules for spoken forms, so that in this domain as well it will make sense to think of the system as an "application" of natural language structure to a new domain.

5 PRESENTATION OF TEXT-CATEGORY INDICATORS

The function of the rules for presentation of category-indicators is to specify a mapping from a representation of the abstract syntactic structure of the text into a class of text-inscriptions (i.e., presentations of the text on a page, a CRT screen, a billboard, or wherever). At a basic level, we can distinguish two different levels of presentation rules. *Linearization rules* map syntactic structures into linear sequences of alphanumeric and non-alphanumeric characters on which are realized all those features of font, face, case and size that are relevant to the identification of text-categories. These rules are at least roughly analogous to the phonological rules that determine the realization of spoken-language structures as segmental sequences, though they are quite different in detail, a reflection of the dissimilarities between the phonetic and alphabetic modes of representation. On the other hand, *pouring rules* have no obvious spoken-language equivalents; these are the rules that map linear sequences of characters into two-dimensional displays in which line-breaks, page-breaks and so forth are realized. At first blush, it might seem as if such rules should not be treated as part of the written language itself, inasmuch as the particular form of a two-dimensional display of a text appears to be independent of its content. (Thus we can repour a text into a new page format, or into a reshaped window on a CRT screen, without changing its linguistic significance.) But as we will see in the final part of this chapter, there are certain text-category indicators that are best treated as features that are inserted as part of the pouring rules, rather than as part of the linearization rules.

The nature of presentation rules depends on two connected considerations: the graphical form of the indicators, and the manner in which they mark category elements and boundaries. Formally, the indicators with which we will be concerned can be realized by any of three graphical devices:

a. By distinct characters, such as the standard marks of punctuation. We will see that it is convenient to distinguish a special class of these called points, which includes the comma, the semicolon, the colon, the period and the em dash.

b. By font-, face- case- and size-alternations (such as the use of italics to mark quotes or citations), and in particular, by capitalization of word-initial alphabetic characters.

c   By the use of "null" elements like spacing to separate text elements like words and lines from one other, or to set text off from the margins or other features of the document format (as required to set off block quotes).

These types are adequate to describe the presentational features associated with all of the text-categories that we will be concerned with here, though other types will be necessary to describe those collateral systems of figural representation that are used along with the categories of written language in the presentation of natural-language documents (e.g., footnotes, captions, headers, tables and so forth).

Functionally, these indicators can mark categories in any of three ways:

a. As *delimiters*, which mark one or both ends of a member of a given category type.

b. As *distinguishers*, which set off a piece of text from its surroundings text in virtue of some distinctive properties of its inscription.

  c. As *separators*, which are inserted between elements of the same category type.

These formal and functional properties are not entirely independent of one another. For example, it is in the nature of distinguishers that they can be realized only as font-, face-, or size-alternations or by underlining or analogous devices. What is more, the form of an indicator may be relevant to how it is treated by the pouring rules that determine the form of the two-dimensional display of text. For example, the spaces that separate words and sentences are not presented at line breaks, and the double line breaks that are used in some styles to separate paragraphs are not presented when they coincide with a page break. By contrast, neither line- nor page-breaks are relevant to the presentation of characters like commas or parentheses, or of elements set off by italics. But there is no simple correspondence between the form of indicators and the functional rules that introduce them. As we already noted, for example, the comma can serve as a delimiter in some contexts, and as a separator in others.

TYPES OF LINEARIZATION RULES

To produce a well-formed string of text, we require several levels of presentation rules. At the most abstract level, syntactic types must be associated with indicator features of the appropriate functional type; i.e., with the appropriate delimiters, distinguishers or separators, as the case may be. This can be accomplished by means of a set of rules of *indicator feature assignment* (IFA rules). These are context-free rules that associate a text-category (e.g., a parenthetical, text-sentence, etc.) with one or more indicator types (e.g., left or right delimiters, distinguishers, and so on), and further associate the indicator type with a particular indicator feature (e.g., "[+left paren]" or "[+alternate face]"). We will write such rules with schemas of the general form:

  $C\ ((I, F)\ldots)$

where C is the name of a category-type, I is the name of an indicator-type, and F is a feature specification. Such rules are interpreted by assigning the relevant indicator feature to the node (of the tree associated with the rule) that dominates the relevant category. The stipulation of indicator type (i.e., separator, delimiter, or distinguisher) is in turn interpreted as determining how the indicator feature is inserted or propagated in the structure dominated by the node.

Let us begin by considering how such rules treat the presentation of delimiters. The rule associated with parentheticals, for example, would have the following form:

parenthetical ((left delimiter, [+left paren]) (right delimiter, [+right paren]))

A general rule associated with the indicator type "left delimiter" will ensure that the feature "[+left paren]" is passed down to the leftmost constitutent of the phrase, and a subsequent realization rule will then ensure that the feature "[+left paren]" is realized by insertion of the character <(> before that element. (In what follows, I will use angle brackets to enclose mentions of indicators.). By the same token, the IFA rule for text-sentences might be written as:[27]

Sentence ((left delimiter [+cap]) (right delimiter [+period]))

The indicator feature "left delimiter" will be interpreted in the same way here, as passing the feature [+cap] to the leftmost element – i.e., the first character of the sentence. (I will deal below with other sentence-final punctuation, such as question marks and exclamation points.) The realization rule for the feature [+cap] will then realize the feature by capitalization of the character to which it is assigned.[28]

---

[27]See below for discussion of other sentence-final punctuation, and of the use of double spaces to separate sentences.

[28]The situation with respect to this rule is in fact somewhat more complicated. When a sentence begins with a proper expression, the feature [+cap] can be regarded assigned redundantly. When a sentence begins with a numeral, on the other hand, the typographical feature [+cap] cannot be realized. According to most style manuals, such sentences are ungrammatical, and must either be rephrased, or the number written out. Finally, there are some proper names (such as *le Carré* and *de Valera*) which begin with "hard" lower-cased characters. If such names are allowed to appear in sentence-initial position – a practice that some style manuals allow

(As I noted earlier, I have no particular brief to make for using the apparatus of feature-passing here, as opposed to some other, formally equivalent device. It is not clear that anything of importance hangs in the balance, all the more since appeals to "naturalness" or economy of representation are not particularly compelling in this domain, where rules are manifestly "artificial" in some sense of the term, and are not responsible to the same canons of learnability to which the rules of spoken-language syntax and phonology must answer.)

Now we can consider the IFA rule for distinguished categories, such as are set off by italics. For example, let's suppose that we can establish a category of "citations" that includes both foreign phrases and mentions of linguistic-expression-types. The IFA rule for this category could then be given as:

Citation (distinguisher, [+alternate face])

In this case, the rule associated with the indicator-type "distinguisher" would pass the feature "[+alternate face]" to all children of the category, and ultimately down to the individual characters of the expression. The realization rule associated with this feature will then flip the value of the feature "[italic]" on each character. (We assume that the feature has a default value of [-italic] in most textual genres). When a cited expression is itself contained within a cited expression, however, the application of the feature [+alternate face] will flip the value of [+italic] to [-italic], as in:

(5.1)   The note said simply, *The bookstore will be out of* Principia Mathematica *until next week.*

The IFA rules associated with separators, by contrast, assumes a regular expression as input. The IFA rule for a sequence of text-clauses, for example, would be given as:

C_t^+ (separator, [+semicolon])

− their initial character will have to be marked with a special feature that blocks the typographical realization of capitalization.

The rule associated with the indicator type "separator" then inserts the indicator feature between the members of any pair of elements of the relevant category-type (see below for a discussion of how spacing is adjusted in such cases). For lexical types like the series, we will assume that the relevant type is a regular expression amenable to independent syntactic categorization; the IFA for such a type will then read:

Series (separator, [+comma])

For the present purposes, I will assume that the explicit conjunction before the last term in a series is treated as a constituent of that term.[29]

As we have observed, the realization rules for indicators such as separator commas, italics and quotation marks must be made context-sensitive, so as to ensure that rules like promotion and quote alternation will be followed. Here again, we will assume that this alternation is handled by means of features associated with the relevant types, which are passed down (and in the case of the promotion rule, up as well) by the relevant IFA rules. Thus the rule that introduces the delimiters on quotations must also assign a particular value to a feature such as "[oddquote]" on the relevant node. Assuming that [oddquote] has a default value of [-oddquote], for example, the IFA for quotations would flip this value to [+oddquote], and pass the feature to all of the children of the node. Subsequent embedded quotations will in turn reverse the feature. The realization rule for quotations will then stipulate that the features [open quote] and [close quote] will be realized as < " > and < " > respectively when the relevant node is marked [-oddquote], and < ' > and < ' > elsewhere.[30]

---

[29]It is a nontrivial matter to ensure that the separator is inserted before a conjunct introduced by an explicit conjunction only when that element is the last in the series, so as to rule out, for example, *We saw Bill, and Sandy, Peter, etc. But I will not deal with this problem here.

[30]Technically, it is true that these alternations could be handled by context-free mechanisms by doubling the set of categories and rules. Such a

It would be possible, of course, to handle all of these alternations by making the IFA rules themselves context-sensitive, but a treatment in terms of two levels of rules will make exposition easier. What is more, this approach makes for a more intuitive description of certain kinds of cross-grapholectal and cross-linguistic variation. Thus we would want to say that the difference between British and American practice with respect to choice of outermost (i.e., "unmarked") quotation marks is due to a difference in the way in which a single delimiter type "quotation mark" is realized, rather than in saying that the two varieties have completely different rules in this environment. By the same token, the distinguisher associated with the category of "mentions" may be realized either by underlining or italics, often according to the writing technology being used; here again, we would like to be able to say that the two practices accord with a single abstract rule.

ABSORPTION RULES

As was noted in the last chapter, several further types of rules are required to ensure the correct presentation of those indicators that are realized as discrete characters – i.e., the standard punctuation marks. In particular, such marks are subject to a number of sequencing constraints. For example, we note that no more than one "point" indicator (i.e., comma, period, semicolon, dash or colons) can be presented in sequence in any given position. We need some rules, then, to tell us which indicator shall be explicitly presented when several syntactic boundaries coincide.

For starters, note that we never get sequences of two commas, In each of the following examples, the location of the "missing" comma is underlined:

(5.2)   Hagy, who had resigned in 1985, in fact, protested the policy.

---

solution would be inelegant, however, and I will not discuss it here; for our purposes, nothing hangs in the balance.

(5.3)   Since August, 1986, when Baltimore was only 2 games out, and fighting for the lead with the Red Sox, the Orioles have won only 81 games.

One way of explaining this regularity is by thinking of the standard punctuation marks as affixes, or better clitics, which attach either rightwards or leftwards to the neighboring word. The comma, for example, is a left-cliticizing mark, and thus in (5.4) the (underlined) initial delimiter comma is presented as attached to the last word of the preceding phrase, despite the fact that it is introduced as a delimiter of the following phrase:

(5.4)   John, who had seen the movie, left early.

For all subsequent purposes, such as line-breaking, the comma is treated as an inseparable part of the word to which it is attached.

I will return to this notion below, in connection with the discussion of the insertion of spaces between words and sentences. For now, however, we can think of the restriction on doubled points as a kind of constraint on word-formation, such that (with certain exceptions) a word can present only one point at a time. When two comma-boundaries coincide, then, only one of the commas will be presented.

On consideration of examples like (5.2) and (5.3) alone, of course, it is difficult to say, and in any event, immaterial, "which" comma is in fact presented. Where feature assignment rules insert marks of different types at the same point in the text, however, their presentation is determined by a set of "absorption" rules that assign them a certain order of precedence. By way of example, note that a comma is never presented when a comma boundary coincides with a boundary marked by a semicolon, colon, dash, or period.[31]

(5.5)   John left, apparently.

(5.6)   John left, apparently; Mary stayed.

(5.7)   John told them the news, apparently: Mary had left.

---

[31]See below for discussion of the special cases of parentheses and quotes.

(5.8)   Among the speakers were John, a linguist; Mary, a lawyer; and Ed.

(5.9)   John had told them the news, apparently — they were forewarned.

In each of these examples, the missing comma is the right-hand delimiter of a lexical adjunct whose right boundary coincides with the right boundary of another phrasal category that dominates it in the syntactic representation of the text. Thus it might be tempting to assume that these regularities are due to a rule that erases or absorbs the innermost bracket when certain sequences of righthand brackets coincide. In the case of the dash, however, the "missing" comma can sometimes be assumed to have wider scope than the indicator that is actually presented:

(5.10)   I am glad you asked me that, my friends – if I may call you that — because I have a good answer.

(5.11)   Jones, who had never seen the pictures – none of the crewmen had — was completely devastated.

It is reasonable to assume, then, that these constraints hold among indicator types, rather than among the types of syntactic brackets that they indicate. That is, we assume that presentation of cliticized indicators is subject to a fixed presentation hierarchy, with the comma at the bottom of the heap.

We can find further support for this notion in several observations. First, note that the left boundary of a comma-delimited element can coincide with the right boundary of an element that is delimited or separated by another point, and that in this case as well the comma is not presented:

(5.12)   John left. Apparently, Mary stayed.

(5.13)   John left; apparently, Mary stayed.

(5.14)   John gave us the news: apparently, no one was coming.

(5.15)   In the opening scene of the play – the scene in which the murder takes place — which scandalized the audience, she makes no appearance.

In these examples, there is no question of determining the precedence of presentation by reference to the relative scope of the categories delimited by the various indicators, and the boundary delimited by the comma must clearly fall to the right of the boundary delimited by the other marks. Thus these regularities could not be stated at a syntactic level by means of the same conditions that govern the appearance of commas in (5.5)–(5.10). But the establishment of an indicator precedence hierarchy will work here equally well; the commas in (5.12)–(5.15) are not presented because the clitic slots on the preceding words are already filled by other indicators that take precedence over the comma.[32]

This same device will enable us to explain the circumstances under which other marks like the dash are presented. We have already noted that the dash takes precedence over (or "absorbs") the comma; note also that the dash is itself absorbed by the period, colon and semicolon.

(5.16)   We heard the sound of their artillery – devastating in its fury.

(5.17)   We heard the sound of their artillery – devastating in its fury: the nine-pounders that had been dragged up from the coast.

(5.18)   We heard the sound of the artillery – those devastating nine-pounders: the battle had begun.

(This constraint applies only to right-delimiter dashes; as we noted earlier, dash-interpolations cannot appear in sentence- or clause-initial position, and so left-delimiter dashes will never have occasion to be absorbed by a preceding period, comma, or semicolon.) Note also that a dash absorbs a following series or sentence-conjunction comma, but is itself absorbed by the semicolon that replaces that comma when promotion has operated:[33]

---

[32]Alternatively, if a sentence like (5.12) is text-initial, the first comma is not presented because there is no prior word for it to attach to.

[33]According to some handbooks, the rule of promotion must apply when an item in series contains internal punctuation of any sort, in which case some of these examples are ill-formed.

(5.19)   *Among his early books were *The Warden, Barchester Towers* –
          that's my favorite, *The Small House at Allington, Dr. Thorne*
          and *The Last Chronicle of Barset.*

(5.20)   Among his early books were *The Warden, Barchester Towers* –
          that's my favorite ₌ *The Small House at Allington, Dr. Thorne*
          and *The Last Chronicle of Barset.*

(5.21)   Among his early books were *The Warden,* in which Mrs.
          Proudie and Mr. Harding first make their appearances;
          Barchester Towers – that's my favorite; *The Small House at
          Allington; Dr. Thorne;* and *The Last Chronicle of Barset.*

(5.22)   John will have to be asked to chair the first session – that
          would be ideal ₌ or we will have to reschedule the entire
          conference.

(5.23)   *John will have to be asked to chair the first session – that
          would be ideal, or we will have to reschedule the entire
          conference.

(5.24)   Either the opening remarks will have to be kept to fifteen
          minutes, or John will have to be asked to chair the first
          session – that would be ideal; or we will have to reschedule
          the entire conference.

Observe that the presence or absence of the dash in these examples
depends not on the nature of the coincident syntactic boundary,
which is the same in either case, but on the particular indicator that
realizes it.

QUOTATIONS AND PARENTHETICALS: BRACKET ABSORPTION

The absorption rules we have outlined will handle most of the
interactions of the point indicators (i.e., commas, semicolons, colons,
periods and dashes), but we require other rules to explain the
interaction of these indicators with parentheses and quotation marks.
We will begin with parentheticals, since quotation marks present
special problems. Note that considerations of relative scope are
relevant to determining whether commas are presented together
with right parentheses. When the insertion points for a comma and a
right parenthesis coincide, the comma is not presented when the

boundary it delimits falls within the scope of the parenthetical, as in (5.25). But it is presented when it marks a boundary that is outside that scope, whether because the comma-delimited element dominates the parenthetical, as in (5.26), or because that element falls to the right of the parenthetical, as in (5.27):

(5.25)   May failed the test (she had not studied the material, which was handed out when she was absent) and will have to repeat the course.

(5.26)   May failed the test, which covered all of the readings (including the book she had lost), and will have to repeat the course.

(5.27)   May failed the test (given on Monday), which covered all of the readings, and will have to repeat the course.

Note that exactly the same regularities govern the interaction of dashes and right parentheses, as in:

(5.28)   May failed the test (which was not surprising – she didn't study) and will have to repeat the course.

(5.29)   May failed the test – which covered all of the readings (including the book she had lost) – and will have to repeat the course.

(5.30)   May failed the test (given on Monday) – I can't say I'm surprised – and will have to repeat the course.

The situation with quotation marks is exactly the same, except that here the interaction with commas is complicated by the rule of quotation transposition (see below), so that it is most clearly exemplified by consideration only of dashes:

(5.31)   *David announced that "the test will be a breeze – you don't have to study – " and went out to play ball.

(5.32)   David announced that "the test will be a breeze – you don't have to study" and went out to play ball.

(5.33)   David was sanguine – the test would be a breeze for which "you don't have to study" – and went out to play ball.

(5.34)   David announced that "the test will be a breeze" — he is always optimistic before the fact — and went out to play ball.

These observations suggest that the co-occurrence of parentheses and quotations with other punctuation is best handled by means of a syntactic rule (which could be formulated as a condition on bracket absorption), which will stipulate that the boundaries of quotations and parentheticals absorb any coincident point-delimited boundaries within their scope.[34]

Note that this rule can be assumed to operate on any point that falls within the scope of a parenthetical or a quotation. Thus quote-internal sentence periods are not presented either:

(5.35)   John went around saying, "The butler did it" to everyone he met that weekend.

But sentence periods are presented when the quotation falls within the scope of the sentence. In American style, of course, these periods are subject to the rules of quote transposition, but an example from British style will make the contrast clear:

(5.36)   Nelson's last words were supposedly 'Kiss me, Hardy'.

We assume, then, that this rule of bracket erasure is purely syntactic; i.e., need make no reference to any hierarchy of indicator-types. It is not surprising that parentheticals and quotations should comprise a separate class with respect to absorption rules, since they have in common the property of being symmetrical paired delimiters (delimiter commas and dashes are paired, but not symmetrical). Note also that these are just the indicators that are not subject to any rules of absorption; both open and close quotation marks and parentheses must always be presented. For this reason, the rule of bracket absorption does not in fact operate on these indicators themselves, despite the fact no ambiguities would be created by its application. Thus there are no semantic consequences to eliminating

---

[34]Note that only delimiter commas are at issue here; for various reasons the point of insertion of a series comma cannot be coincident with the insertion point for a colon, a semicolon, or a higher-level parenthetical.

the right parenthesis in (5.38a), or the right quotation in (5.38b), but the results are nonetheless syntactically ill-formed:

> (5.38a)   John said, "We must do our duty (or somebody's)"; no one answered.

> (5.38a')   *John said, "We must do our duty (or somebody's"; no one answered.

> (5.38b)   Horace moped in without a word (he was in what he called his "blue funk") and flopped down on the bed.

> (5.38b')   *Horace moped in without a word (he was in what he called his "blue funk) and flopped down on the bed.

QUOTE-TRANSPOSITION AND OTHER MATTERS

We have already mentioned the American rule of quote-transposition, which transposes (any number of) quotation marks and a following period or comma, but which does not operate on semicolons, colons or other marks. Thus the most widely-accepted American style requires:

> (5.39)   Nelson actually said, "England *confides* that every man will do his duty."

> (5.40)   Nelson actually said, "England *confides* that every man will do his duty," but the message was changed by the signal officer.

> (5.41)   Nelson actually said, "England *confides* that every man will do his duty": the message was changed by a signal officer.

> (5.42)   Nelson had only one audience in mind when he said, "England expects that every man will do his duty": posterity, not the fleet.

Note that this rule of quote-transposition must be stated as a condition on indicator types, rather than in purely syntactic terms, inasmuch as it does not apply when series elements are separated by semicolons rather than commas, even though the syntactic boundaries are of the same type in either case:

(5.43)   He repeated all the great naval mottoes: Nelson's "England expects that every man will do his duty," John Paul Jones' "I have not yet begun to fight," and Commodore Perry's "We have met the enemy and he is ours."

(5.44)   He went through all the great naval mottoes: Nelson's "England expects that every man will do his duty," which is actually a misquotation; John Paul Jones' "I have not yet begun to fight"; and Commodore Perry's "We have met the enemy and he is ours."

It is particularly instructive to see how the rule of quote-transposition interacts with the presentation of other indicators.[35] For one thing, it helps to shed light on the nature of the question mark and the exclamation point – the "tone indicators" – which I have not considered up to here. It is generally assumed that such marks are sentence-final delimiters, alternatives to the period. But while it is certainly true that periods are not added to sentences terminating with either of these marks, there are problems with this analysis, since tone-indicators can appear in various sentence-internal positions in which periods are not tolerated:[36]

(5.45)   Hail source of being! universal soul!

---

[35]The rule itself is considerably more interesting in British style, where its correct application traditionally requires a sensitivity to the sense of the sentence. Thus Partridge and Fowler recommend alternations like the following:

(i)   Some people insist that Nelson's last words were really "Kismet, Hardy".

(ii)   "This policy," he said, "will bring the government to ruin."

where the difference between (i) and (ii) could be described in terms of whether the quoted sentence makes the "primary" assertion of the sentence. In recent years, however, the British appear to be moving more towards a categorical rule.

[36]Note that in these examples, the material associated with the tone-indicators cannot be assumed to consist of "suppressed" quotations:

(i)   ?They knew the attack was coming, but "when?" and "from where?"

(5.46)   They knew the attack was coming, but when? and from where?

Note, moreover, that unlike other points, tone-indicators are not absorbed when they occur within sentence-internal parentheticals and quotations:

(5.47)   The attitude expressed by "Am I my brother's keeper?" is quite prevalent in today's America.

(5.48)   Their questions (when was the test due? who would grade it?) were natural enough under the circumstances.

(The distributions of the question mark and the exclamation point are exactly parallel, so that it will not be necessary hereafter to exemplify all the uses of both.) Finally, note that points like the comma, semicolon, colon and dash occur freely following the tone-indicators, but never before them:

(5.49a) What we want to know is when?, but he has told us only why.

(5.49b) *What we want to know is when,? where,? and how?

(5.50a) What we want to know is when?; until you answer that question, we cannot come to a decision.

(5.50b) *Who could do it;? when would they start?

(5.51a) What we want to know is when? – up to now you've told us only why – and until you answer that question, we cannot come to a decision.

(5.51b) *Who could get away with it – not John, surely – ? and why would anyone want to?

In this respect, the tone indicators behave as if they were right paired symmetrical delimiters (which of course they are in languages like Spanish).

There are several observations that suggest a more plausible alternate analysis of the tone-indicators. First, we note that a sentence period is not presented when the sentence concludes with a quotation terminating with a tone-indicator, but that it is presented when the sentence concludes with a parenthetical terminating with a tone-indicator:

(5.52)   I am puzzled (who is he?).

(5.53)   I am annoyed (he is a fool!).

(5.54)   I asked her, "Who is she?"

(5.55)   I told her, "He is a fool!"

In British style, by contrast, the final period in sentences like (5.54) and (5.55) can be presented (though the practice is often condemned in the handbooks on purely graphical grounds; as we noted, British practice does allow transposition in certain circumstances).

(5.56)   His exact words were, "Who is she?".

(5.57)   I told her, "He is a fool!".

It is plausible to assume that the period in (5.54) and (5.55) is absorbed by the tone-indicator, once it has been placed inside the quote by quote-transposition; the obligatory presentation of the period in (5.52) and (5.53) would then follow from the fact that transposition does not operate across parentheses, so that the conditions for a rule of absorption would not be satisfied.

Such an absorption rule would be particular to the period, of course; as we noted, commas and other marks can occur after tone-indicators. But there is independent evidence for the existence of a rule of just this sort. Note that a sentence period does not appear when the last word of a sentence is an abbreviation:

(5.58)   He lives in Washington, D. C.

(5.59)   The star of the Oak Hills High School team last year was Pete Rose Jr.

By contrast, other marks occur freely after the abbreviation period:

(5.60)   It requires a sentence period; i.e., a full stop.

(5.61)   He lives in Washington, D. C.; she lives in New York.

In fact, the abbreviation period can even precede the tone-indicators themselves, unlike all other points:

(5.62)   Are you going to Washington, D. C.?

Like hyphens and apostrophes, the abbreviation period is an indicator of word-structure, rather than of text-structure, and so figures at a wholly different level of analysis from the indicators we have been considering. The hyphen, for example, can be regarded as an affix that attaches to a word-part, rather than to a word, and as such it does not interact with any of the indicators of syntactic categories:

(5.63)   These are paragraph-, sentence-, or clause-boundaries.

But the rule that requires the absorption of the full stop by a preceding abbreviation period would be plausible as a purely graphical constraint, which makes reference to sequences of mark-types, rather than to sequences of indicator-types. And inasmuch as the realizations of the tone-indicators are graphically a kind of annotated period, the extension of this rule to cover sequences of <?.> and <!.> would have the same motivation.[37]

In that case, there is no longer any compelling reason for assuming that the tone-indicators are sentence-delimiters at all; the fact that they appear to "replace" the full stop is explained by an independent constraint. Rather, we can think of them as annotations which can be attached to an element of any type, and which are

---

[37]We might expect, then, that this rule would apply to sequences of colons and periods, as well. And in fact there is a bit of evidence for this assumption, if we consider the presentation of colon expansions that consist of a set of sentences and paragraphs, as in:

(i)   There are several things we have to do before the conference starts: Bette has to prepare the brochures. Someone should make sure the registration tables have been ordered from Facilities.

(ii)   We propose a three-part program designed to address these problems:

           First, a committee will be formed with the task of deciding on a policy for new equipment acquisitions. . . .

It is possible to argue that the first sentence of (i) and (ii) concludes with the colon, in which case the absence of a sentence-final period would be better explained by reference to a graphical constraint than by introduction of a special rule for use of the colon. But as I noted in the previous chapter, these examples are problematic, and I will not press this point here.

entirely orthogonal to the categories of text structure. Unlike the other marks of punctuation, the tone-indicators really are interpreted by reference to intonational patterns in the spoken language, and the elements they delimit are best thought of as tone-groups, rather than as syntactic categories.[38]

ORDERING OF LINEARIZATION RULES

We have up to here identified five kinds of rules that must be assumed to operate on the output of feature assignment rules to produce correct strings of indicated text. These are:

Realization rules, which associate features with indicator types;

Point absorption rules, which determine which of multiple point indicators (i.e., commas, semicolons, colons, dashes and periods) will be presented when these indicators coincide at a given insertion point;

---

[38]Note that this will help us in explaining an otherwise curious observation about the use of such indicators. As we observed, question marks and exclamation points can occur before semi-colons, as in:

(*i*)   What we want to know is when?; until you answer that question, we cannot come to a decision.

Note, however, that question marks do not occur at the end of an initial text-clause when the question intonation is interpreted as extending over the entire clause, and when the sentence does not involve a series of parallel questions:

(*ii*)   *Is he coming?; that's what we would like to know.

(*iii*)   Is he coming?; are we going?; is everybody staying home?

Rather than explaining this restriction by means of some syntactic apparatus, which would be implausibly cumbersome, we might better suppose that (*ii*) is unacceptable on purely tonal grounds; that the "rising tone" associated with the question in the first clause of (*ii*) is inconsistent with the "falling tone" generally associated with the first clause of a sentence consisting of two semicolon-separated elements. For that reason *wh*-questions are somewhat more acceptable in this environment:

(*iv*)   (?)What does he want?; that's what we would like to know.

As I noted earlier, these "tones" are of course never spoken except by the mind's mouth, and their nature is psychologically mysterious; I will not push this line of speculation here.

Bracket absorption rules, which eliminate all point-indicated boundaries that occur within the scope of paired symmetrical delimiters (i.e., quotation marks and right parentheses);

Quote transposition, which transposes close quotation marks and following periods and commas; and

Graphic absorption rules (period absorption), which cause a full stop to be absorbed by an immediately preceding abbreviation period, question mark, or exclamation point.

Throughout our discussion, we have further assumed that these rules must be at least partially ordered with respect to one another (or equivalently, that the rules must be structured so as to give the effect of ordering; the difference will not be important here). The ordering is as follows:

Realization rules
Point absorption rules
Quote transposition
Graphic absorption

(The relative ordering of bracket absorption cannot be decisively determined.)

Some of the arguments for this ordering have already been presented. Realization rules must precede both point absorption rules and quote transposition, since both of these are sensitive to distinctions (such as between commas and semicolons) that are not available until after the realization rules have applied. By the same token, we know that transposition must precede graphic absorption, since that ordering is required in order to ensure that the sentence-final periods will be absorbed in examples like:

(5.64)   He asked, "Are you coming?"

(5.65)   She said, "I'm going to Washington, D. C."

It remains to determine the ordering of point absorption rules and quote transposition. In this connection, consider the following examples:

(5.66)   She came in her truck, which she called "li'l red"; it was a blue Toyota.

(5.67) She came in her truck, which she called "li'l red" – though it
was big and blue.

Prior to the application of either point absorption or transposition,
we will assume that these sentences have "underlying
representations" roughly as in the following (spacing should be
ignored in these examples):

(5.68) She came in her truck, which she called "li'l red",; it was a
blue Toyota.

(5.69) She came in her truck, which she called "li'l red", – though it
was big and blue.

If transposition were to apply before point absorption, we would be
left with representations as follows:

(5.70) She came in her truck, which she called "li'l red,"; it was a
blue Toyota.

(5.71) She came in her truck, which she called "li'l red,"– though it
was big and blue.

In that case, the conditions for point absorption would not be
satisfied, and so we could not refer to that rule to explain the
absorption of the commas.

It might be argued, of course, that the absorption of the comma
in (5.66-67) is in fact the consequence of a subsequent application of
the bracket absorption rule, which absorbs all point-delimited
boundaries internal to a closing quote. But transposition affects only
the order of indicators: there is no reason to suppose that it has any
effect on syntactic boundaries.[39] And in any event, bracket

---

[39]This can be seen from the way transposition interacts with italicization.
Consider, for example:

(i)   *I don't know who said *Damned be he who first cries* "Hold, enough,"
and I don't care. (comma and close quote italicized)

where transposition will have operated to place the comma within the the
italicized citation, and the comma is thus presented as italicized. If
transposition did in fact change the relative scope of the comma and the
citation, we would expect this sentence to be acceptable. On the other hand,
the version of (i) in which the comma is not italicized is equally

absorption must be presumed to apply before transposition, in order to generate the correct punctuation in a sentence like (5.72):

(5.72)   "Sentimentality‚" Wilde said, "is the attribution of tenderness to nature where God did not put it."

We assume that (5.72) has an underlying representation as suggested by (5.73) (again ignoring spacing):

(5.73)   "Sentimentality"‚ Wilde said, "is the attribution of tenderness to nature where God did not put it."

If transposition preceded bracket absorption, we would then expect the comma to be absorbed, leaving us with:

(5.74)   *"Sentimentality" Wilde said, "is the attribution of tenderness to nature where God did not put it."

We assume, then, that the commas in (5.66–67) could be absorbed only by the rule of point absorption, and hence that this rule must apply before transposition.

This leaves us with a scheme of rule-ordering that mirrors the general ordering properties – and no less interesting, the complexity of interaction – that we observe in the phonological systems of spoken language. The earliest rules are those that make reference to abstract syntactic features. Subsequent rules make reference to indicator types (i.e., commas, semicolons, periods), and then to indicators considered as graphical elements. Thus we infer that no explicit statements about ordering need be included in the grammatical description of presentation rules.[40]

---

unacceptable, inasmuch as italicization cannot apply to the discontinuous constituent created by transposition:

(ii)   *I don't know who said *Damned be he who first cries "Hold, enough‚"* and I don't care. (comma not italicized, close quote italicized)

[40]To be sure, there is no particular reason to suppose that these rules must be formulated in terms of discrete levels, though I have done so here for ease of exposition. It would be possible to recast the rules given here, for example, in terms of various other notational systems that are available to describe spoken-language morphology and phonology.

NULL SEPARATORS AND POURING RULES

The last set of presentation rules that I want to take up here are those that insert null-element separators (that is, blank spaces and line breaks) between words, sentences, and paragraphs.[41] As I noted earlier, these rules are different in important respects from the presentation rules for other delimiters, and are best handled in a different way.

For purposes of argument, suppose we were to introduce these separators by means of the same devices we used to introduce separators like the semicolon that occurs between text-clauses. Then we would include among the feature assignment rules such rules as:

Word$^+$ (separator, [word space])

Sentence$^+$ (separator, [sentence space])

paragraph$^+$ (separator, [para break])

The features "[word space]," "[sentence space]" and "[para break]" would then be interpreted by realization rules as sequences of a space, a double space, and a line break respectively.

But there are several problems with this approach. First, the introduction of these rules at this level would complicate the statement of rules of cliticization, if they applied together with the realization rules for commas and other points. That is, we would have to provide rules to transpose left commas and spaces, and some analogous devices to ensure that separator commas and semicolons wound up on the right (which is to say, left) side of the spaces adjoining them. Obviously it would be easier to assume that insertion of spaces took place after cliticization of commas and other marks.

The second problem involves only word-spacing. The type "Word$^+$" occurs in the text-grammatical representation only as an expansion of the text-phrase. Thus this rule would provide for the insertion of spaces between words where no other text-syntactic

---

[41]In typographic or electronic media, of course, this "null" element is in fact a character, but I have used the standard linguistic terminology on the assumption that spaces are perceived as the absence of a character, and that it is this perception that what is relevant to their distribution.

boundary was present, but we would have to add additional rules to insert separators between text-phrases and text-clauses of various types. Such rules could of course be reduced to a small number of statements with the judicious use of features, but the need for multiple rules is still doubtful.[42] Intuitively, we would like to be able to say that the word-spacing rule is a single entity which ignores all sentence-internal boundaries, and which treats all boundary indicators indifferently as parts of the words onto which they have been cliticized.

Finally, as we have noted, the rules for insertion of null separators interact in a complicated way with the rules for "pouring," which determine the form of the two-dimensional display of text. In the first place, certain of these separators, such as the newlines used to separate paragraphs and the margin changes that set off block quotes, cannot be physically realized in the linear text-string at all. As such, they would have to be represented in the linear representation of the text by abstract features, which would be subject to an independent set of realization rules that formed part of the pouring rules.

What is more, all of these null-elements are sensitive to the presence of line-breaks and page-breaks in the two-dimensional display. Thus word- and sentence-spaces are not presented when the boundary they mark coincides with a line-break, and double-line spacing between paragraphs (as used in business letters, for example), is not presented when the paragraph boundary coincides with a page-break. (By contrast, the pouring rules have no effect on the presentation of non-null indicators like punctuation marks and font- and face-alternations.) If word- and sentence-spacing were already present in the linear representation of the text, then, we would have to make provision for deleting line-final spaces in the process of pouring.

---

[42]Note that these could not be reduced to a single rule, which inserted spaces as separators for all types of the form X^+ or some such, inasmuch as the expansion of lexical and text-phrases into heads and adjuncts could not be described using a regular expression of this type.

For all of these reasons, it makes more sense to think of the rules for null-separator insertion as applying in conjunction with the other rules of pouring, after linearization rules have applied. We will assume that pouring rules operate on a linear text structure in which only the types word, sentence and paragraph are represented (where the word is understood as containing all cliticized indicators, so that phrase- and clause-boundaries present no special problems). We will also assume that the rules for insertion of null-separators operate only within certain graphically-defined domains, such as the line (for word- and sentence-separators) and the page (for paragraph separators in business-letter style). The rules of null-separator insertion will then stipulate that single spaces be inserted between line-adjacent word-boundaries; that double spaces be inserted between line-adjacent sentence-boundaries; and that newlines be inserted between page-adjacent paragraph boundaries.[43]

It is important to keep in mind the distinction between these rules considered as linguistic characterizations and the various kinds of layout rules used by writers, typographers or computational systems in actually producing two-dimensional layouts of text on a page or screen. These latter processes are "graphetic," like the rules that determine those properties of the font, face, and size of characters that are not relevant to the indication of written-language categories. What is more, both pouring rules and layout rules may interact with other sorts of figural conventions that are collateral to the general system of written-language text-grammar. (For example, we noted that a line break can figure as a category indicator in lists and tables, as well in linguistic genres such as poetry.) Finally, I make no claim as to the way in which these pouring rules are in fact embodied internally in people or systems. In at least some cases, in

---

[43]In the discussion above, we treated a sentence boundary as being a word-boundary as well, so as to be able to generalize the absorption of left-delimiter-commas that occurs in examples like:

(i)   She left. Apparently, he stayed.

This suggests that there are really two different spaces inserted at sentence boundaries: one as a word-separator, and the other as a sentence-separator.

fact, it is clear that they cannot have the form we have outlined here.[44]

TEXT-CATEGORY PRESENTATION RULES IN CONTRAST

We have looked at a number of different sorts of rules that are relevant to the presentation of indicators: realization rules (notably as relevant to quote alternation and comma-promotion), cliticization, rules of absorption, and rules of transposition. It is in the form of these rules, more than in the rules of syntax, that the particular character of the text-grammar emerges. When we contrast them with the rules of natural-language phonology and morphology, we can see how the text-grammar reflects the fact of its figural, rather than phonic, presentation. When we contrast them with the presentation rules and notational conventions associated with analogous constructed graphical languages – that is, with linear alphabetic languages like those of mathematics and logic – we see how the text-grammar reflects its use as a part of a natural-language system, which must be processed and interpreted in an efficient way, as part of the activity of linguistic comprehension. In this chapter, I will try to draw some of these contrasts anecdotally, bearing in mind that a thorough and systematic comparison is beyond the scope of this monograph.

In many cases, there is simply no analogy between the rules of indicator presentation and the rules of spoken-language phonology. (There is obviously nothing in phonology, for example, that can be compared to the presentation rules concerned with two-dimensional display.) Elsewhere, however, we may be tempted to draw various parallels, inasmuch as both modes are essentially segmental. For example, the rule of quote transposition has a clear analogue in

---

[44]In a character-level editor like EMACS, for example, separator spaces will be represented between all pairs of words in the text-stream, subject to a condition that ensures that they will not be presented, or will be presented invisibly, at line breaks. The system could not do otherwise, inasmuch as it is capable of "representing" a word-boundary only as a space character. In a natural-language structure editor, by contrast, it would be possible to represent such syntactic information directly, and state the conditions on presentation of word-separators in a manner more like that suggested here.

phonological metathesis. But even in these cases we must proceed with caution. Phonological metathesis generally serves the purpose of easing the articulation of consonant clusters or of bringing syllable structure in line with a certain canonical form.[45] But such explanations of the role of metathesis depend crucially on the fact that phonetic processes are directional, in accordance with the ballistics of articulation. so that a sequence of two phonetic segments will be easier to produce or perceive when pronounced in a one order than in another. Whereas the presentation of text-category indicators is subject to no such considerations of relative difficulty of transition between segments in production. Even in texts in which lexical material is written cursively, indicators like the period and the quotation mark are always written as discrete segments, so that there is no greater manual difficulty in writing $<X.">$ than in writing $<X".>$.

To be sure, typographers have sometimes said that the American practice of transposing quotes and points has an aesthetic motivation: that the sequence $<X.">$ is somehow either more pleasing or easier to perceive than the sequence $<X".>$, which leaves an ungainly space beneath the quote. (The rationale for this judgment is that a space before a point is regarded as aesthetically objectionable, whereas a space after a point is aesthetically satisfying. But if carried to a logical conclusion, this principle would mandate the transposition of quotation marks and semicolons and colons as well, or conversely, the transposition of periods and apostrophes.) Granting the truth of this observation (and it would seem that the testimony of typographers is more conclusive here than any experimental evidence could be), we can say that both phonetic and graphic metathesis have their motivations in general principles of production and perception. But there is no instructive analogy to be drawn between the particular perceptual principles that motivate the

---

[45]I am ignoring the use of metathesis as a morphological (i.e., meaning-bearing) process, as in various Semitic languages. Such processes could have no analogues in the text-grammar, since individual indicators appear never to be realized by sequences of more than one segment, and so could not have variant forms in which the order of segments is reversed.

rules in one or the other domain, and so the formal resemblance between the two processes is not especially significant. It indicates only that transposition of segments is always an available option in segmental languages, for whatever reason.[46]

The same kinds of differences between phonetic and graphic processes underlie other differences between rules of phonology and text-category indicator presentation. For example, the rule of point absorption appears to resemble various phonological processes that result in the simplification of various sequences, as when the first of a series of two non-homorganic stops is not realized, or is assimilated to the second. In fact the general principle that only one (graphical) stop may presented in a particular clitic spot has an obvious analogue in various constraints on canonical syllable structure. But there are important discrepancies between the two types of rules, which are directly related to the fact that the process of transcription of indicators is not subject to the same principles of directionality that operate in phonetic and phonological processes. Thus the modern-day rule of point absorption requires that a dash take precedence over a comma, whatever their relative order or scope. By contrast, we would not expect to find a rule of cluster simplification in which such sequences as /pt/ and /tp/ were both realized as /t/ or /tt/ whenever they occurred, or a rule in which a the voicing of a fricative was assimilated to that of an adjacent homorganic stop on either side of it.[47] By the same token, we would not expect to find a morphological rule that stated, for example, that affix A was never realized in conjunction with affix B, in whatever order the two

---

[46]In this connection, McCawley (ms) has observed that metathesis-like processes are found in formal languages like that of mathematics, where the expressions that might more "properly" be written $(\sin x)^n$ are more often written as $\sin^n x$, thereby rendering parentheses superfluous. McCawley's article offers an interesting linguistic perspective on the notational conventions of two types of constructed graphical languages, and I have borrowed some of his observations in the discussion below.

[47]It has occasionally been argued that such "mirror-image" rules exist in phonology, but the phenomena that might support such analyses are at best marginal in the world's languages, and are more often analyzed as involving independent rules. See Anderson (1974) for a discussion of this question.

happened to appear, whenever affix A was realized by a particular phonological shape.[48] Finally, it is not surprising that the rule of point absorption has no analogue in rules determining the distribution of intonational contours, the spoken-language features which are functionally closest to text-category indicators, but which are of course realized non-segmentally. Thus a particular intonational pattern A may "absorb" another pattern B that is associated with a string that falls within its scope, but we would not expect it to absorb B when B is associated with a following segment.

The rule of point absorption also provides a good point of comparison between the presentation rules for text-category indicators and the notational conventions of analogous constructed graphical languages. The motivation for absorption rules, we assume, is in the fact that sequences of indicators may be difficult to produce or process, and may be informationally redundant relative to the linguistic and extralinguistic context of their interpretation. And of course constructed languages incorporate various notational conventions designed to achieve the same effect. Often, it is true, constructed languages accomplish this by means of devices that would be cumbersome or inappropriate for natural-language texts, such as by defining a certain order of application among operators, or making use of superscripting and analogous devices to do the

---

[48]This formulation is required in order to draw the analogy at the morphological level, since the "same" graphical affix (e.g., a lexical separator) may take two forms (as a comma or semicolon), and will either absorb or be absorbed by a dash accordingly. Thus let us suppose that X is a stem, and that A and B are both suffixes, such that A has variants α and a that are determined by independent phonological or morphological processes. To find an analogue of point absorption, we would have to find the following distributions:

$X + \alpha + b \rightarrow X\alpha$

$X + b + \alpha \rightarrow X\alpha$

$X + a + b \rightarrow Xb$

$X + b + a \rightarrow Xb$

This seems to me a highly unlikely set of alternations.

work of association.[49] But other notational conventions used in formal languages have effects that are more directly comparable to

---

[49]For example, we understand the expressions in the (a) versions of ($i-$ ii) to be equivalent to the bracketed expressions in the (b) versions:

(ia) $a + b * c$

(ib) $a + (b * c)$

(iia) $b * c + a$

(iib) $(b * c) + a$

(iiia) abc

(iiib) $a(bc)$

In general, however, it is hard to imagine how conventions of this sort could be applied to do most of the work that text-category indicators do in natural-language texts, given the difficulty of identifying "operators," and in determining the boundaries of categories that are not explicitly marked in some way. The one case in which this option would be at least theoretically available would be in the use of separators to indicate scopal relations among conjuncts, as variously in (iv) and (v):

(iv a)   John will chair the first session or Mary will chair the second, and no one will chair the third.

(iv b)   John will chair the first session, or Mary will chair the second and no one will chair the third.

(va)   John will chair the first session, or Mary will chair the second; and no one will chair the third.

(vb)   John will chair the first session; or Mary will chair the second, and no one will chair the third.

In principle, one could define a relation of precedence among conjunctions in sentences like these such that the differential use of separators was unnecessary: say by saying that the leftmost conjunction was interpreted as having widest scope. It is unlikely, however, that any language would adopt so (linguistically) unnatural a convention simply to get out of having to write a comma now and again.

In addition, mathematical and formal languages make extensive use of devices like superscripting and subscripting to type expressions, as in expressions like 3^{2}. These devices do in fact have analogues in the natural-language use of indicators like font-and face-alternations, but the applicability of such devices is limited both by the graphical means at the disposal of the writer and the difficulty in reading texts inscribed in such a manner. Thus it is logically possible that one could replace all of the those of natural-language presentation rules. For example, various conventions allow the omission of brackets either where where no ambiguity would result, as with the outermost brackets of the expression in (5.75a), which is equivalent to (5.75b). Or brackets may be omitted where the ambiguity created is benign, as in (5.76a), which given the associativity of addition, might be interpreted indifferently as equivalent to (5.76b) or (5.76c):

(5.75a) $a + (b - c)$

(5.75b) $(a + (b - c))$

(5.76a) $a + b + c$

(5.76b) $a + (b + c)$

(5.76c) $(a + b) + c$

Conventions like these do have analogues in natural language texts, notably in the optionality of the use of certain commas, or of the promotion rule, when the indicators are not required to disambiguate scope relations among conjunctions and other constituents. Thus a comma is optional in (5.77), but obligatory in (5.78), where it restricts the scope of the prepositional phrase *while in office* relative to the disjunction:

(5.77)   Every president since then has died(,) or has become ill.

(5.78)   Every president since then has died, or has become ill while in office.

---

indicators in a sentence like (*vi*) by face- and font-alternations, say by using sans-serif type for comma-delimited phrases, italics for italics, bold for parentheticals, and superscripts for dash-interpolations, as in (*v ii*) :

(*vi*)   He assigned Silas Marner – a book that Jean, who spoke little English (and read less), could barely understand.

(*vii*)   He assigned *Silas Marner* ᵃ book that Jean who spoke little English **and read less** could barely understand ᵂᵉ ʳᵉᵃᵈ ⁱᵗ ᵃⁿʸʷᵃʸ·

Such conventions appear to make the processing of text quite difficult for the reader of running text. Note however that they come into their own when we leave the text grammar proper to look at other aspects of natural-language document design. (For a survey of such devices, see Norrish (1987).)

By the same token, promotion is optional in a sentence like (5.79), since conjunction, like addition, is associative; but it must apply in a sentence like (5.80):

(5.79)   Jack will chair the first session, and Mary will give the opening address, and Bill will make the closing remarks.

(5.80)   Jack will chair the first session, and Mary will give the opening address; or Bill will make the closing remarks.

I have not said anything here about the optionality of various punctuation marks, since it affects exclusively the use of punctuation as an indicator of lexical structures, an area that I have in general avoided in this discussion. Note, by contrast, that there is no optionality in the use of clausal indicators like the dash, the colon, or the parenthetical. Thus we cannot omit the final parenthesis in (5.81), despite the fact that in American English, the parenthetical could not in any case extend beyond the sentence boundary:

(5.81)   *No other option exists (though some may continue to hope. We will simply have to bite the bullet).

Note moreover that optionality does not extend to the use of more than one point where a lexical structure would otherwise be ambiguous. Thus (5.82a) is ambiguous with respect to whether the relative clause is restrictive or nonrestrictive, but a comma cannot be used to disambiguate the structure, as in the ungrammatical (5.82b):

(5.82a) She would not meet the salesperson, however, who had no appointment.

(5.82b) *She would not meet the salesperson, however,, who had no appointment.

By the same token, the (modern) promotion rule can apply only once to disambiguate a conjunction: a sentence like (5.83), for example, is beyond the power of the text-grammar to fully disambiguate by further promotion:

(5.83)   Either Jack will chair the first session or Henry will chair the third, or Mary will give the opening address, and Bill will make the closing remarks; and Ellen will chair the second session, but no one will chair the third.

The closest analogue to the rule of point absorption in constructed languages is probably in the notational conventions whereby a particular symbol or bracket can be used to obviate the inscription of series of redundant brackets, such as the close square bracket of Interlisp, which is interpreted roughly as an instruction to "close all the relevant parens." Thus (5.84a) is interpreted as equivalent to (5.84b):

(5.84a) $(a(b(c])$

(5.84b) $(a(b(c)))$

But this rule too is different from the rule of absorption in several important respects. First, it cannot be applied where any syntactic ambiguity would result (if it could, it would not compile); in such cases, sequences of brackets must be used. Whereas the rule of point absorption is obligatory, even when the resulting string is syntactically ambiguous. The difference between the two reflects a well-known and important difference between formal languages and natural languages, in that the latter are much more tolerant of syntactic ambiguities.[50] Given the availability of the lexical and extralinguistic contexts to perform much of the work of disambiguation, the explicit marking of all category boundaries would be informationally redundant in many cases, and hence not particularly desirable. It is for this reason that natural languages can get away with grammaticized procedures like the absorption rules, which embody what is probabilistically a relatively optimal solution to the problem of minimizing both sequences of brackets and pernicious ambiguities, and which can be applied mechanically.

Note moreover that tolerance of ambiguity is built not only into the absorption rules, but into the system of text indicators itself. For example, it uses the the same marks (commas) as left delimiters,

---

[50]Though it has often been remarked that mathematical and programming languages do permit more ambiguities of various sorts than is generally acknowledged. See, e.g., McCawley (ms.) for some examples of the former.

right delimiters and separators, and it provides no indicators at all for certain boundary types, such as the right bracket of a colon-expansion. Given the available means for marking category boundaries, sentences of the form of (5.85) and (5.86) cannot be syntactically disambiguated, even if no rule of absorption is involved:

(5.85) $A: B; C.$

(5.86) $A, B, C.$

Thus in (5.85) the semicolon could have wide or narrow scope with respect to the colon; and in (5.86) the commas could be interpreted as delimiting a lexical adjunct B, or as separating A, B and C as items in series. But in actual texts, ambiguities of the first type will be quite rare, and ambiguities of the second type will be virtually non-existent.

This point is related to a second difference between the Interlisp square bracket convention and the rule of absorption. The Interlisp bracket is interpreted directionally: it delimits only those categories lying to the left of it. In this respect it resembles the rules of bracket absorption associated with parentheses and quotation marks, but not the rules of point absorption, which can operate, for example, to ensure that a semicolon or dash will absorb the left boundary of a comma-delimited element lying to its right. In theory, of course, it would be possible to introduce into Interlisp a second, analogous convention involving the use of an open square bracket to mean "open all relevant parens," as well as a notational convention that abbreviated the two brackets with a single symbol, so as to have a mark that at least seemed to function like a semicolon under the text-grammar rules of point absorption. But such a convention for use of the open bracket would be undesirable, since it would require a forward search of indeterminate length to locate all the relevant closing brackets.

But this observation raises a central question about how readers in fact process the indicators that figure in the point absorption rule. As we have seen, this rule requires that the semicolon in a sentence like (5.87) and the rightmost dash in (5.88) must be analyzed as absorbing the left delimiter of a lexical adjunct (that is, a left comma boundary):

(5.87)   No one passed; ncxt June, everyone will have to take the exam again.

(5.88)   Everyone seems to recall that the officer – or so he styled himself – who boarded at Vigan, had a curious accent.

But at the same time, it is highly unlikely that readers must determine whether such absorption has takcn place in the course of processing the underlined indicators in these examples, precisely because such processing would itself require a forward search of indeterminatc length. (Recall that we argued in the last chapter that analogous assumptions about processing would explain the impossibility of a natural-language rule of quotation alternation in which the unmarked form was assigned to the most deeply embedded, rather than the leftmost, quotation.) Thus in both examples, the determination that the underlined indicator represents the left boundary of a lexical adjunct can be made only once the right delimiter comma of the adjunct has been encountered (assuming there is no context to aid in disambiguation). Note, moreover, that this problem does not affect only the absorption of comma boundaries that follow the delimiter. In (5.89), for example, we cannot determine whether or not the underlined dash has absorbed the closing comma boundary of the relative clause until we have processed the final phrase of the sentence.

(5.89)   The state party nominated Gray, who opposed the war – he was a conscientious objector, in fact – but supported the national platform, as their candidate for Mayor.

Whatever the actual manner of processing of the indicators these examples, then, let us assume that it does not require the resolution of all indicator ambiguities (or more accurately, all category-boundary ambiguities) at the point where they occur.

This assumption enables us to account for several basic observations about the system of text-category indicators, as realized at all historical stages and in all languages that use it. First, point absorption is always a categorical rule; that is, sequences of two or more stops are never tolerated.[51] Second, certain sets of distinct syntactic functions appear always to be associated with particular indicators: for example, the comma is always used as both a separator and delimiter of lexical phrases, and is the semicolon is always a separator. These observations suggest that there is a general unitary processing strategy associated with each stop, which provides partial information about the boundary associated with it, and which interacts in a complex way with the processing strategies associated with the content of the associated text-categories and lexical constituents to yield a satisfactory interpretation of particular sentences.

This suggestion accords with the intuitions that underlie the discussions of stops in the traditional literature, where a particular type of indicator is almost always associated with a particular and singular juncture phenomenon. Until the nineteenth century, grammars and handbooks tended to describe these juncture phenomena by reference to the lengths of the pauses they were perceived as indicating (it was this perception, of course, that led to their classification as "stops" in the first place). In some cases, such as Bishop Lowth's influential grammar of 1762, the various types of juncture were associated with hierarchically organized text-syntactic types:

> The several degrees of Connexion between Sentences, and between their principal constructive parts, Rhetoricians have considered under the the following distinctions, as the most obvious and remarkable: the period, colon, semicolon, and comma. The period is the whole Sentence, compleat in itself, wanting nothing to make a full and perfect sense, and not connected with a subsequent Sentence. The colon, or Member, is a chief constructive part, or greater division, of a Sentence. The semicolon, or Half-member, is a less constructive part, or subdivision of a Sentence or Member. A Sentence or Member is again subdivided into commas, or Segments; which are the least

---

[51]The status of the dash as a point has tended to fluctuate. Until the twentieth century, points were sometimes used before the dash, though never following it, and there are some nineteenth-century styles in which the dash can be regarded almost as a diacritic that emphasizes the mark with which it is associated.

constructive parts of a Sentence, or Member, in this way of considering it; for the next subdivision would be the resolution of it into Phrases and Words.

The Grammarians have followed this division of the Rhetoricians, and have appropriated to each of these distinctions its mark, or Point; which takes its name from the part of the Sentence which it is employed to distinguish, as follows:

The period is thus marked .

The colon is thus marked :

The semicolon is thus marked ;

The comma is thus marked ,

The proportional quantity or time of the Points with respect to one another is determined by the following general rule: The period is a pause in quantity or duration Double the colon: the colon is double of the semicolon; and the semicolon is double of the comma. So that they are in the same proportion to one another as the Semibrief, the Minim, the Crotchet, and the Quaver, in Music.

This is an elegant scheme, in which the length of the pause associated with each stop is determined by the hierarchical role of the text-constituent-boundary it indicates. If the picture were true, it would provide a perfect explanation for the observations we are interested in here. The obligatory nature of point absorption would follow from the fact that a series of short pauses cannot be distinguished from a single long one, and that a pause that announces the end of a category cannot be distinguished from one that announces the beginning of another.

Unfortunately, Lowth's description must be taken with two grains of salt. First, the structure of the text-grammatical categories was not so simply hierarchical as he suggests, though it is true that the functions of the semicolon and colon were then more general than they are now, as their use in this passage itself indicates. Second, we can be assured that the pauses and the relations among them were only phenomenal (all the more since silent reading was likely to have been a widespread practice among the literate classes by this date). Later expositions of the junctures associated the points have tended to describe them in terms of a more abstract scale of "weight," or as Partridge (1953) puts it, "value": he assigns to all the stops a relative value as follows, "based on a fundamental 10 for a period":

parentheses	1 or 2
comma	2 or 1
dash	3-5
semicolon	6
colon	8
period	10

(Note that Partridge, like Lowth, is describing the earlier practice in which the colon is used as a higher-level separator than the semicolon.) Of course this scheme is no less fantastical than Lowth's, particularly since Partridge never says what sort of stuff these numbers are intended to quantify. But the basic intuition behind both schemes is almost certainly sound. For that part of the natural-language processor associated with text-categories, it is probably sufficient that each of the points be associated with a very general type of category boundary, or perhaps more accurately, with a certain general type of juncture. The full repertory of types that we have described here would then be derived from the association of partial information about these boundaries with various information about the lexical content of the associated text-elements. Thus it may be that text-grammar processing makes use of a set of types that is no more elaborated than those that Lowth presents, so that distinctions, say between separator commas and and delimiter commas are not represented as differences between two kinds of commas, but rather fall out as theorems from the combination of a unitary type of comma boundary with various kinds of lexical phrases.

There remains the question of why the indicators associated with certain categories, in particular the quotation and the parenthetical, should be necessarily symmetrical and paired, so that with these categories we require an explicit indication of both the beginning and end of the category. Two reasons come to mind. First, as we will see below, both quotations and parentheticals can straddle the boundaries of lexical constituents, and as such their boundaries tend to be less predictable on the basis of lexical information than those of other types. Thus in (5.90), we could open the quotation at any of the points indicated by a single quote:

(5.90)   According to the Senator, 'the 'entire 'shooting match 'is 'hanging by a thread."

Second, we will see in the following chapter that quotations and parentheses have certain semantic properties in common, and that arguably the determination that certain lexical material is parenthetical- or quote-internal could not be "put on hold" in the course of sentence-processing.[52]

These remarks on the processing of text-category have necessarily been tentative, but they should be sufficient to make the general points I am after: that the presentation rules of for text-category indicators are distinct from the rules of spoken-language phonology in their essential reliance on a figural, rather than a phonic substance; and that they are distinct from the notational conventions of constructed languages in their reliance on a processor that can take advantage of the various sorts of redundancies and cross-dependencies that are always available for natural-language texts.

---

[52]Note that while the point absorption rule has been categorical for the entire history of the modern punctuation system, the rule of bracket absorption is a more recent development. In an 1811 edition of *Clarissa*, for example, we find commas occurring before close parentheses (and delimiter commas before open parentheses), as in:

> We are indeed more afflicted with the news of your being so very ill than I can express ; for I see not but, after this separation, (as we understand that your misfortune has been greater than your fault, and that, however unhappy, you have demeaned yourself like the good young creature you used to be,) we shall love you better, if possible, than ever.

This suggests that bracket absorption is in fact a more superficial rule, in the sense that it is more like the notational conventions of a constructed language than like the rule of point absorption, which on this account reflects the fundamental organization of the text-grammatical processor.

6 The Functions of Text-Categories

Now we can turn to the purposes that the text-grammars have arisen in order to serve. The system of text-categories serves to classify the relations among expressions of written texts along several orthogonal dimensions, which have in common primarily the fact of their special relevance or importance to the written genres in which the system has evolved. To do full justice to the description of these relations, we would have to be able to build on general accounts of the structure and ontology of written discourse genres, of the social context of written communication, and of the organization of document types in which texts are inscribed. This would be a tall order, which I will be making no effort here to fill. Instead, as in previous chapters, I want to try to give the flavor of the enterprise by discussing examples of the function of two sorts of text-categories, which will demonstrate how the system of text-categories responds to the exigencies of written communication, and will allow me to make some concluding observations about how the functions of text categories are integrated in the system of text-grammar.

ARGUMENT-STRUCTURE CATEGORIES

Argument-structure categories include the the text-sentence and the paragraph, as well as a number of genre-specific categories like the section and the chapter. Typically, these categories function to provide partial information about the role of the the interpretations of linguistic expressions relative to what I will call the argument of the text. Roughly speaking, the argument of a text is the thing it refers to or describes: a structured domain that could be characterized as a model, a situation, a set of worlds, or whatever. Just what particular sort of object the argument is depends on the particular genre at issue. To take a relatively straightforward example, the argument of a recipe is what we may call a procedure, which in turn consists of hierarchically organized constituents that we could call sub-procedures, operations, and so forth. Somewhat more tentatively, we could say that the argument of a conventional narrative history or novel is what we may call a story, which consists of hierarchically organized episodes, events and the like. But these characterizations would become problematic if we examined them more closely; and when we come to other genres, such as an elaborated exposition or demonstration, it is hard even to attach a name to the argument of the text. Fortunately, we do not have to deal with the ontology of arguments in order to be able to describe the relations among their parts or the way in which those parts correspond to the text-elements that describe them.[53]

Essentially, the argument-structure categories of the text-grammar perform two related roles: they serve to classify linguistic expressions according to the sorts of argument-elements they describe, and to indicate certain hierarchical relations among those expressions that correspond to the hierarchical organization of elements in the argument domain. Let me start with this second function, which is perhaps more obvious and easier to describe.

The process of interpreting a text involves associating the interpretations of its lexical constituents with elements of its argument. When we read a recipe, for example, we recognize in virtue of our prior knowledge of the genre that certain expressions (typically, imperative lexical sentences) are to be interpreted as descriptions of the basic operations that constitute the procedure that the recipe describes, and that these expressions must be associated with one another in a manner that allows the reconstruction of

---

[53]It makes no difference here which approach we take, though it would be difficult to describe the role of argument-structure categories if we were to extend the classical view of (lexical) sentence reference to complex (declarative) texts, and say that they denoted only truth-values.

higher-order constituents of the argument, such as complex operations, sub-procedures and the like. It is of course possible to transcribe a recipe in such a manner that text categories provide no information about the hierarchical organization of an argument, say by enumerating lexical sentences in the form of a list, as in:

(6.1)   preheat the oven to 350°

oil a shallow baking pan that will hold the fish nicely

wash the fish and pat dry

set aside

put the shrimp through a food grinder

combine with egg, salt, pepper, sherry and cream add vegetables. . .

In this case, it is left entirely to the reader to infer the hierarchical relations among the elements of the argument. In another context (for example in a spoken discourse) we might supply further information about such relations by explicit lexical stipulation, e.g. by saying such things as "That takes care of the goose sauce; now for the gander," or more simply still, by the use of various lexical conjunctions. In a written (running) text, however, we have also available the option of using the hierarchical categories made available by the text-grammar, say by inscribing the lexical sentences that describe operations as text-sentences, and grouping together in separate paragraphs descriptions of operations that constitute a single sub-procedure, as in:

(6.2)   ¶Preheat the oven to 350°.

¶Oil a shallow baking pan that will hold the fish nicely. Wash the fish and pat dry. Set aside.

¶Put the shrimp through a food grinder. Combine with egg, salt, pepper, sherry and cream. Add vegetables. . . .

Such categories will rarely provide all relevant information about hierarchical relationships among text elements, nor is such explicitness generally required; in addition to the system of hierarchical text-categories, the reader can refer to explicit lexical signals and to plausible strategies of inference to reconstruct the organization of the argument.

The other function of text categories is so obvious that it is easy to overlook: structural categories also serve to classify linguistic expressions according to the kinds of elements they refer to in the argument domain. The structural categories of the text-grammar are not entirely an empty hierarchical scheme that can be imposed on the lexical expressions of the text in an arbitrary way. In the preceding example of a recipe, for instance, we naturally assumed that the imperative lexical sentences that described simple operations of the procedure should be inscribed as separate lexical sentences. But we might have conveyed exactly the same hierarchical information had we inscribed the lexical sentences as semicolon-conjoined text-clauses, and used text-sentence boundaries, rather than paragraph boundaries, to indicate distinct sub-operations, as in (6.3):

(6.3)   ?¶Preheat the oven to 350°. Oil a shallow baking pan that will hold the fish nicely; wash the fish and pat dry; set aside. Put the shrimp through a food grinder; combine with egg, salt, pepper, sherry and cream; add vegetables.

Clearly (6.3) represents an unconventional way of transcribing a recipe, but what exactly is the convention that it flouts? As a first pass, we might say that (6.3) fails to respect the general rule that in the unmarked case, each lexical sentence shall be inscribed as a separate text-sentence. This is true as far as it goes, and it does touch on the heart of the matter, which is the observation that the categories of lexical sentences and text-sentences are related functionally, as well as etymologically. But we have to have a better understanding of what the "unmarked case" is, and of when and why we tolerate departures from this norm: when a text sentence consists either of a non-sentential lexical expression (what the handbooks call a "sentence fragment") or, what is more important, of a string of concatenated or interpolated lexical sentences connected by semicolons, colons, or other sub-sentential indicators.

These are important questions, for as I suggested earlier, the relation between the text grammar and the lexical grammar is encapsulated in the relation between the two notions of "sentence."

The convention that links the two is best cast in terms of conditions imposed on the reference of text-sentences: text-sentences refer to the *basic elements* of the argument of the text. The nature of the basic elements depends on the genre: in a recipe, they are simple operations; in a narrative they are individual events; and so on.

Now the basic elements of the arguments of the genres we are particularly concerned with here – the operations of a recipe, the events of a narrative, the steps of a demonstration – are essentially the same kinds of things as the entities described by lexical sentences of various types (which I will take here to be things like actions, situations, and states of affairs). But they are further subject to conditions of registration and criteria of individuation that are particular to the specific genres involved. Thus the operations of a recipe are actions registered as instructions or steps, and individuated according to the interests, the resources and the presumed level of expertise of the reader. The events of a narrative are situations registered and individuated according to their role in a certain causal chain (as opposed, say, to the events of a chronicle like a police log, which need have no causal interconnection).

Note that the practice of using lexical sentences to express the elements of argument structure is prescribed by the conventions of particular genres. There are many natural-language written genres that conform to other practices. Thus the basic elements of a (simplified) dictionary are pairings of lexical items (conventionally expressed by citation forms) and senses (expressed by lexical elements of the appropriate categories: noun phrases for nouns, infinitival phrases for verbs, and so on). In theory, these elements could be expressed by text sentences like *The meaning of* ineffable *is first, "incapable of being expressed in words," and second, "not to be uttered"* and so forth, but such a representation would be neither efficient nor graphically perspicuous for purposes of search and retrieval. By the same token, we could imagine a genre in which the events and episodes of a novel would be represented in a table that associated the names of characters with predicates and with integers that indicated the ordering of events in the story, though such a system would be somewhat unwieldy. More realistically, there are certain kinds of information (some instructions, for example) that can be represented in either fashion. It is a question of great importance for the theory of written documents to ask just which properties of a genre make it desirable to use lexical sentences as the expressions of the situations, actions, or states of affairs that are registered as basic elements of argument structure, but that is not a question I can go into here. For the present, let us simply accept that there is a particular class of *sentential genres,* in which basic elements of the argument are characteristically composed of the interpretations of lexical sentences.

THE USES OF SEMICOLONS

In a sentential genre, to inscribe a lexical sentence as a text-sentence is essentially to classify it as describing a single basic element of argument structure. In the simplest case, there will be a one-to-one mapping between the interpretations of lexical sentences and the basic elements of the argument, and hence a one-to-one mapping between lexical sentences and the text-sentences that describe those elements. But it is also possible that the criteria that individuate argument elements should be different from those that individuate the interpretations of lexical sentences. Thus we may regard a single operation in a recipe as corresponding to two or more actions, or a single event in a narrative as corresponding to two or more situations. As we noted earlier, the text-grammar makes available various syntactic devices for signalling such composition; most simply, by allowing lexical sentences to be conjoined as text-clauses in sentences like (6.4):

(6.4)   She told him the truth; the others lied.

It will be worth spending a little time examining this construction, for it can help to shed light on the classificatory function of the text-sentence, and more generally, on the way in which the text-grammar is used to relate the interpretations of lexical expressions to the units of discourse structure out of which various written-language genres are composed.

We interpret sentences like (6.4) by assuming that the interpretations of the text-clauses must somehow be combined or composed to form a single argument element of the relevant (basic) type. The differences in the final interpretations of such constructions depend on the particular inferences that allow this composition. In some cases, we will simply assume that the basic element consists of the conjunction of the interpretations of the constituent text-clauses. This is the reading associated with a sentence like (6.5), for example:

(6.5) ¶Meanwhile, in a saute pan, over medium heat, cook lobster and shallots in 1 ounce olive oil for 2 minutes; remove lobster.

In (6.5), we assume that the operation described by the first sentence consists of the conjunction of the actions described by its constituent clauses: that is of cooking the lobster and removing it. (This conjunction could equally well have been expressed by an explicit lexical coordinator, of course, in which case we would have treated the interpretation of the text-sentence as an atomic unit.)

The question then arises why we should want to consider these two actions as parts of a single operation, rather than as distinct operations. The answer depends on how we are individuating basic elements of the argument of the genre in question. In recipes, operations are generally understood as composed of actions or sets of actions that have in common the time, place and often the manner of their performance, or the function they serve (though there can be a fair amount of latitude in how these criteria are implied, inasmuch as recipe writers can presume more sophisticated compilers than programmers can). In the case of (6.5), the assumption that the actions described by the two text-clauses might lead to the inference that they are to be performed within the same time period, and hence that the lobster should be removed immediately after cooking. In other examples, the same considerations may lead to the resolution of scopal ambiguities, such as are often occasioned by the highly elliptical nature of the lexical syntax of recipes:[54]

6.6a. Wash the fish. Pick over the crabmeat. <u>Remove the cartilage and flake the meat; set aside</u>.

---

[54]For these purposes, we can ignore the elliptical style of the language of recipes; for discussion, see Culy (ms).

¶In a 12-inch skillet, bring the stock to a boil. Add the fish, cover, reduce heat.

The punctuation of (6.6a) entails that the implicit object of *set aside* is the crabmeat, and not both the crabmeat and the fish (as made clear in the following paragraph, which calls for the fish in the next sub-procedure). Note that this reading would not have been forced if the two clauses were inscribed as separate sentences, as in (6.6b):

6.6b.   Wash the fish. Pick over the crabmeat. <u>Remove the cartilage and flake the meat. Set aside.</u>

To account for this restriction, however, we do not have to assume that the text-grammar imposes any direct conditions on the anaphoric relations that can hold among lexical elements (conditions that would be both difficult to state and theoretically uncongenial). Rather, the restriction follows from the inference that the conjunction of the actions described by the semicolon-connected clauses constitutes a single operation, spatiotemporally distinct from the operations described by the preceding text-sentences. This inference would not be justified if the action of setting (something) aside were to be construed as applying both to the crabmeat and the fish, since there would then be no distinguishing commonality between that action and the action of removing the cartilage and flaking the crabmeat that warranted treating the two actions as a single basic element of the procedure.

We find this same general pattern of inference associated with many uses of semicolons in other genres, as well. Consider (6.7), for example, from a narrative history:

(6.7)   ¶And Woolworth's flourished. <u>By 1900 his volume was over $5 million a year; in another five years it had trebled.</u> For more customers he reached up into the middle classes. [Daniel Boorstin]

Let us say that the relevant elements of the argument structure in (6.7) are events, which are individuated according to their causal role with respect to other events. Thus the use of the semicolon in the underlined sentence requires us to construe the interpretations of the two text-clauses as constituting a single event. In context, we can satisfy this requirement by assuming that the event consists of the conjunction of the interpretations of the clauses, in which case the evidence for the fact that Woolworth's had flourished is assumed to consist of the fact that volume was at $5 million a year in 1900 *and* that it had further trebled by 1905. Note that the alternative reading, wherein the evidence of flourishing consisted simply of the fact that volume was at $5 million a year in 1900, would have been in principle available if the two clauses had been inscribed as separate sentences, as in:

(6.8)   ¶And Woolworth's flourished. <u>By 1900 his volume was over $5 million a year. In another five years it had trebled....</u>

Note however that this conjunctive reading is only one way of satisfying the requirement that the text-sentence describe a single element of argument structure. In other contexts, we may prefer to read the semicolon-conjoined text-clauses as providing alternate descriptions of a single object of the relative type. This is the pattern of interpretation associated with sentences like (6.9)–(6.11):

(6.9)   Devein the shrimp; slice the shrimp along top of shell and remove vein.

(6.10)   Her every sentence sang itself to a melody so thin-lipped, so emptily affected, so bloodless, so heartless, so senselessly and conclusively complacent, that it was not merely inhuman but inanimate, not merely lifeless but the negation of life – as you listened plants withered, the landscape grew lunar, the existence of paramecium, of molds and spores, of the tobacco mosaic virus came to seem the fantasy of some utopian planner; her voice said that there is nothing. (Randall Jarrell)

(6.11)   These too are boom jobs; they are dependent on government programs, and they are very largely for women.

In each of these examples, we will satisfy the requirement that the text-sentence refer to a single basic element of the argument by assuming that the two clauses count as descriptions of the same thing. Thus the action of deveining the shrimp is taken to be the same as the action of slicing the shells and removing the veins; and the state of affairs described by saying that her every sentence sang itself to a thin-lipped melody is the same as the state of affairs described by saying that her voice said that there is nothing. Against the background of this assumption about the interpretations of the clauses, we can interpret their discourse relation in any of several ways. Depending on the order of clauses, and the kind of description they provide, we may say that one clause counts as an elaboration or explanation of the other, or as a summary. But we should keep in mind that the determination of coherence relations like "elaboration" and "summation" in fact depends on determining two kinds of relations among linguistic expressions, the one a relation between the interpretations of the expressions (relative to which there is no difference between elaboration and summation), and the other a relation between the informational content of the expressions, which supplies further distinctions. Thus while assumptions about the relations between the interpretations of text elements cannot fully determine the nature of the discourse relation that holds between them, such assumptions can constrain the selection of the discourse relation. This is how the semicolon works, and why, doubtless, grammarians have been tempted to describe its function in terms of its discourse role, or the particular set of coherence relations it can express, though this last is in fact only an indirect consequence of its syntactic role.[55]

---

[55]Standard handbooks explain the uses of semicolons in one of two ways: by saying that they "join parts of a sentence that are too closely connected to be made into distinct sentences," as one puts it, or by saying that they "can be used to replace any missing coordinator" (Meyer 1987). In both cases there is an implication that the semicolon implicitly constrains the semantic relation that holds between the clauses. (Note that this formulation is typical of most treatments of the semantics of punctuation, which assign the semantic value to the marks, rather than to the structures they indicate.) In the abstract, however, the set of relations that can be inferred between two semicolon-conjoined clauses is exactly identical to the set of relations that can obtain between separate sentences. Thus in the absence of context, (i) and (ii) have the same readings:

(i)   One went to Texas; the other went bad.

(ii)   One went to Texas. The other went bad.

We can demonstrate this point in connection with another, related pattern of interpretation associated with semicolon-conjoined clauses, as exemplified in (6.12)–(6.14):

(6.12)   Nothing seemed to go right. When the Earl of Denby, the great magnate of Lancashire, landed from the Isle of Man to bring his followers to the King's aid, he was instantly defeated at Wigan. <u>The presence of Commonwealth spies in the Royalist organization exacerbated its problems; Isaac Birkenhead, a supposed Royalist agent, betrayed the correspondence between the King and Lord Denby.</u>

(6.13)   In general, the Commissioners of Parliament satisfied everyone with their becoming deference; the reference of Denzil Holmes to the twenty years' tyranny of Cromwell was particularly moving.

(6.14)   Even writers one thinks of as relatively abstruse and shy at one point or other followed the lecture trail; Henry James toured the States coast to coast in 1904 and 1905 lecturing on "The Lesson of Balzac," and Melville for a time in the late 1850's. . .sought to generate the income that his books were increasingly failing to supply by speaking, at fifty dollars a lecture, on "Statues in Rome" and "The South Seas." [John Updike]

In (6.12), we assume that the underlined text-sentence must be read as describing a single "thing that went wrong," and hence that the states of affairs described by the two clauses must belong to the same state of affairs: more specifically, that the state of affairs described by the second clause (the betrayal of the correspondence) is part of the

---

As we have seen, the difference between strings of lexical sentences inscribed as semicolon-conjoined clauses and those inscribed as separate text-sentences emerges only relative to a particular context, where the use of the semicolon may constrain the choice of the relation to a subset of the relations available for discrete sentences. But this follows not from any particular relational meaning assigned to the semicolon, but to the interpretation that is assigned to the subordinate structure that it signals.

state of affairs described by the first clause (the exacerbation of the army's problems by the presence of spies). In the circumstances, we assume that the second clause is offered as an exemplification of the general condition described by the first.

I won't try here to give an account of the full range of readings of text-grammatical constructions of this form, not only because such a demonstration is unnecessary, but because it raises questions that are more relevant to theories of the organization of discourse in general and to the underpinnings of semantics than to the particular uses of text-category indicators. For one thing, we don't have adequate framework for talking about many of the relevant notions (for example, it is not clear how to reconstruct formally the intuition that underlies our saying that one situation or state of affairs is "part of" another.) But the preceding discussion should be adequate to show in a general way how argument-structure categories like the text-sentence and paragraph are used to classify the interpretations of linguistic expressions according to their role in the structure of the argument that the text describes.

It is important to note that by itself, this function is not unique to the categories of text-grammar of written language. On the one hand, there are many devices in the spoken language that serve to indicate structural relations among elements of the discourse. Some of these, like explicit lexical indicators, are available in both written and spoken modes; others, like intonational contours and prosodic features, are restricted to speech. To be sure, these devices are not precisely equivalent to the argument-structure categories of the text-grammar, nor would we expect them to be, given the fundamental differences in the presentational substrates in which writing and speech are realized, and the differences in organizational complexity between the kinds of genres that are customarily consigned to the two modes. For example, we would not expect the intonational system of the spoken language to provide devices that do for us the work of larger argument-structure categories like the section or chapter, since the genres of spoken discourse do not ordinarily involve units of this size. As a purely practical matter, moreover, the intonational resources of speech are not usually called upon to regiment discourse units of the internal complexity that written-language sentences can sometimes achieve, a point I'll return to below. But by themselves these observations do not reflect a difference of kind between the discourse-structure signalling devices of written and spoken language, but only of degree.[56]

On the other hand, the functions of the argument-structure categories have analogues in the uses of various non-linguistic graphical systems of representation that are used in the inscription of texts of other, non-sentential genres. Thus the items of a list can equally well be treated as argument-structure categories; and if provision is made for recursive embedding of sublists and enumeration of items, we will have the kind of topic outline with which, in principle, the structure of any sentential text can be represented.

The particular interest of the text-grammatical system of argument-structure categories, and of the text-sentence in particular, lies not simply in their function, but also in the way that such categories provide the domain for the syntactic and graphic integration of a system of categories whose functions are complementary to these. But in order to make this point, I will first examine the function of one other type of category, and then consider how such disparate functions are integrated in the text-grammatical system.

CONTEXTUAL CATEGORIES

Contextual categories are really a kind of annotation of text-elements that indicate how their content is to be construed relative to a certain default hypothesis about the relation of the text to the context. One example of such a category is the quotation, which indicates that its linguistic content is to be construed as produced in a different context from that of the production of the embedding text. For our purposes, it does not matter whether the author is quoting himself or

---

[56]There are arguably structural devices of commensurate complexity in specialized oral forms, such as determined by the metrical and stanzaic organization of poetry. I have no interest in arguing here that the system of discourse-structure markers in written language is more complex than the analogous resources of spoken language, but only that it is qualitatively different.

another, or whether he himself endorses the content of the quotation. Nor does it matter whether the content of the quotation is in fact drawn from another text or utterance, as opposed to being ascribed, say, to a hypothetical context (as when someone writes, "As when someone writes 'good morning' on the blackboard.") If we consider the quotation as a univocal linguistic type, in fact, it is a mistake to suppose that it imposes any special conditions on the *reference* of the expressions it contains, or to assume that the paradigmatic use of the quotation is its use in pure mentions of other expressions. Rather, the content of quotations is primarily distinguished from the surrounding text by the distinct circumstances of its production – from which it may of course *follow* that its terms do not in fact refer as they would if then were produced in the embedding context of production.

I don't want to try to give a full-blown account of the uses of quotations here, since too many other issues hang in the balance that are extraneous to our immediate concerns. Rather, I raise the example of quotations primarily to contrast their function with that of another contextual category, the parenthetical, which while far less well studied than the quotation is actually more central to an understanding of the relation of a written text to its context of interpretation.

Standard handbooks describe the parenthetical as used to present "amplificatory, explanatory, or digressive elements." This is true but vague; it does not suffice to distinguish the parentheticals from many other elements set off by dashes, commas and other delimiters. Yet there are important differences between parentheticals and these other text-categories. One way of demonstrating this is to look at the way the material introduced in parentheticals is treated for purposes of application of various syntactic and semantic processes. Note, for example, that elements within parentheticals cannot serve as the antecedents for external anaphors or analogous elements, as shown in (6.15)–(6.20):

(6.15) She came in carrying a loaf of bread and a jug of wine, and set them on the table.

(6.16)   She came in carrying a loaf of bread – and a jug of wine – and set them on the table.

(6.17)   *She came in carrying a loaf of bread (and a jug of wine) and set them on the table.

(6.17)   John won at Indianapolis – and Mary came in second at Daytona – in the same car.

(6.18)   *John won at Indianapolis (and Mary came in second at Daytona) in the same car.

(6.19)   They were serving caviar, so Jonas, who hates parties, went anyway.

(6.20)   ??They were serving caviar, so Jonas (who hates parties) went anyway.

But it would be a mistake to interpret this restriction as the result of a constraint on anaphoric processes imposed within the lexical grammar itself (indeed, as we noted, it is difficult to see how lexical rules could make reference to any sort of text-categorical information). Rather, we can account for these observations by reference to the semantic function of parentheticals, which ensures that their content is not actually incorporated into the text proper, and so is unavailable for any external reference. Thus parentheticals cannot be used to introduce entities that will figure in subsequent discussion – not just pronominal antecedents, but technical terms or personal names:[57]

(6.21)   ??Languages like these (which linguists call "agglutinating") are quite common. Agglutinating languages are found. . .

(6.22)   ??They handed us over to a detective (whose name, ominously, was Frame). We asked Frame whether we would be allowed to go back to the hotel.

---

[57]Note however that a parenthetical can be used to introduce an abbreviation whose interpretation could be derived (though perhaps at greater effort) from a consideration of the non-parenthesized text, as in:

(i)   Let us refer to this as the Second Affix Principle (henceforth SAP). The SAP operates to. . .

Nor can the material in a parenthetical trigger external punctuation that would not be required if the material within the parenthetical were not present. In 6.23, for example, a parenthetical-external hyphen has been triggered by a parenthetical-internal element, with an ill-formed result:

(6.23)   *Assume that *bu'* is locally (Chomsky)-adjoined to V^0.

In short, the content of a parenthetical must be entirely irrelevant to the syntactic or semantic well-formedness of the surrounding text.[58]

From these observations we can deduce the function of the parenthetical. Strip a text of its parentheticals, and you are left with a coherent and complete communication, what we can think of as a primary or *presumptive* text (a term I'll explain in a moment). Thus if the content of the parentheticals is to figure in interpretation, it must be relative to some other circumstances of interpretation, which are distinct from the context associated with the primary text. But in order to flesh out this claim, we have to have clearly in mind the

---

[58]This point is suggested by some traditional handbook formulations of the rule for using parentheticals. For example, Charles C. Boyd writes in *Grammar for Great and Small* (1928): "The test of a parenthesis is whether the other words make sense without it." But as we have seen, the well-formedness conditions extend to considerations of syntactic form, as well as of meaning, and of course the well-formedness of a parenthetical cannot be determined entirely on the basis of a consideration of the well-formedness of the surrounding text. As we saw earlier, for example, a (text-category) parenthetical will be ill-formed if it precedes its head.

I should add one further qualification to these observations about the irrelevance of the parenthetical to the semantic and syntactic well-formedness of the embedding sentence. There may be cases in which the inclusion of a parenthetical adversely affects the acceptability of a sentence, as in (*i*) and (*ii*):

(*i*)   John is planning to attend.

(*ii*)   ?John (and perhaps his wife) is planning to attend.

I am inclined to say that (*ii*) is grammatical, though construal of the parenthetical here may create some problems for the parser associated with these structures. Certainly (*ii*) is preferable to (*iii*), where the embedding sentence would be ungrammatical without the parenthetical:

(*iii*)   *John (and perhaps his wife) are planning to attend.

differences between the characteristic contexts of published texts and the typical context of face-to-face communication that has traditionally served as the paradigm case for analyses of indexicality and context-dependence in philosophical and linguistic approaches to natural language.

THE CONTEXT OF WRITTEN TEXTS

Analyses of the role of context in face-to-face conversation ordinarily proceed under the assumption that the relevant contextual roles (that is, "speaker," "addressee," "time of utterance," "place of utterance," and so forth) are filled by unique, determinate particulars, and hence can be satisfied extensionally. Thus the addressee of a conversational utterance (e.g., the referent – or more precisely, the index – of a token of the pronoun *you*) is simply the particular person or persons to whom it is directed. By the same token, the "agent of the context," as some have called it (that is, the referent of a token of the pronoun *I*) is the very person who utters the token. And so on: the time of utterance (e.g., the time indexed by a token of *now*) is just the unique time of production or processing of the utterance (there being in the prototypical case no relevant difference between the two). Most basically of all, the utterance itself is taken to be a unique event. Having taken face-to-face conversation as the model of communication, linguists and philosophers have therefore felt justified in describing the meaning of the utterance as a relation between those very objects – that very person, that time, and so on – and the situation the utterance describes.[59]

---

[59]This is not to say that the business of interpreting the utterance does not depend in part on a reconstruction of participants' own implicit representations of the relevant contextual features; for example the beliefs and intentions that the speaker ascribes to the hearer and vice-versa, or the particular registration of the time or place of utterance that is relevant to assigning an interpretation to a token of an indexical like *now* or *here* (which is what will determine whether an utterance of a sentence like *Joan is here now* is to be interpreted as meaning something like "Joan is in this city this week" or "Joan is in this room this minute"). But these are beliefs about or registrations of particular persons, places and times that are directly accessible to the participants' experience; i.e., beliefs about *that* person, *this* time, and so on. And for this reason, as a number of people have observed,

When we consider the context of interpretation that is ordinarily relevant to the interpretation of a public written text, however, the nature of such contextual elements as "agent," "addressee" and so forth becomes more problematic. The uncertainty begins with the multiplication of utterances or enunciations, either in the reproduction and dissemination of the text, or in the re-presentation of a unique inscription (such as an airport sign) to a series of individuals. In such circumstances we cannot speak of a unique and determinate time or place of interpretation, nor can we identify a unique and determinate addressee. At the same time, the multiple agencies involved in the production and dissemination of the text, together with the multiplicity of personae that the "author" of a text can assume, make the reference of a "first person" pronoun no less complicated.

An example will help to underscore the relevance of this point. When we read the first sentence of *Huckleberry Finn* – "You don't know about me without you have read a book by the name of *The Adventures of Tom Sawyer*; but that ain't no matter" – we may be hard put to assign a value to the indexical *you*, and hence a set of truth-conditions to the sentence (let us set aside for now the confounded problem of the speaker's own identity, as well as the fact that *Huckleberry Finn* is in fact a fictional discourse). It is often said that the addressee of a text like this one is an "ideal" or "intended" reader, which is to say that the reader is a construct in the author's mind. In that case, we might say that the referent of *you* in this sentence is a representative reader that Twain envisioned, who has bought a copy of the novel just after its publication in 1884, and hence who could know about Huck only if he had read *Tom Sawyer*. This analysis accords with our own experience in interpreting the text; certainly when we modern readers pick up *Huckleberry Finn* we don't think of Huck (or Twain) as addressing someone like

---

these beliefs and intentions do not wholly determine the meaning of the utterance. To adapt an example of John Perry's, if someone says to me, "You entered Paris triumphantly," under the belief that the person he is talking to is Charles de Gaulle, then what that person has said is false.

ourselves, who may know all about Huck Finn without having read Tom Sawyer, either from having seen the any of the five movie versions or from having read the essays of Mr. Leslie Fiedler. (Nor, more important, do we imagine that either Huck or his creator would think of ascribing to his reader such attitudes and beliefs as the abomination of slavery, which we take as part of our own moral landscape.) In interpreting the book, in fact, we may have to imagine ourselves as the sort of reader that Twain had in mind, merely to make sense of the text.[60] Thus the reader is as much a construct for us as Huck is. But Twain's intended reader is not a fictional character, but an idealized individual whose identity is in some sense determined by the circumstances of the presentation of the document: its time of publication, its manner and place of dissemination, and so forth. In this sense there is no difference between the intended or ideal reader of *Huckleberry Finn* and that of a road sign that says *You are entering Bedford Falls*, which again presupposes certain conditions of interpretation – for example, that the interpreter is not someone looking over his shoulder on the way out of town.

Let us call this individual the *presumptive reader* of a text, and by extension, let us refer as well to the presumptive author, presumptive time, place and so on of the presumptive context of a particular text. (I choose this term because the term "intended reader" raises well-known difficulties about the role of the authorial intentions in fixing an interpretation. At the same time, the terms *ideal* and *idealized* are apt to lead to confusions between the circumstances to which the text is actually adapted and the "best possible" circumstances of interpretation. Thus the writer of a logic text might wish for an ideal reader who would follow every demonstration with a minimum of redundancy, but he will be well-advised – by his publisher, if by no one else – to address himself to the beliefs and background of the typical member of the audience he is aiming to reach, which is to say the presumptive reader.) If we then turn the formulation around, and begin with a particular set of presumptive contextual indices, we may speak of the presumptive

---

[60]On the notion of the reader as "fiction," see Ong (1987).

text as the text that is designed to be optimally interpreted relative to those indices.

I don't want to get involved here in trying to say what sort of objects the elements of presumptive contexts really are (that is, whether and how the first sentence of *Huckleberry Finn* might make a true statement). What is important is that while the writer constructs a text under certain assumptions about the presumptive context, he is generally aware that the actual circumstances of interpretation will often be different from those that he has envisioned, and that in the course of interpretation, his actual readers will have to reconstruct the presumptive context on the basis of assumptions about the text and its manner of presentation. (This holds equally for both presumptive and non-presumptive readers. The reader who sees the sign *You are entering Bedford Falls* on the side of the road ahead of him as he is driving into town must be able to determine that the sign is in fact addressed to him – though it is important to note this process need not require the construction of an explicit representation of the context.) In one sense, to be sure, this is true even of face-to-face conversation, in the sense that the speaker will design his utterance in the light of assumptions about his hearer's beliefs and so forth. The difference is that the writer of a public text is assured that no particular set of assumptions about the context could possibly be satisfied across the set of different circumstances in which the text will be encountered; the presumptions he arrives at may be optimal, but cannot be said to be "correct." Thus an ideally designed conversation need make no provision for the possibility the context may be other than it is, whereby an ideally designed text may have to do so. Hence the particular usefulness in public writing of the parenthetical, a device that enables the writer to accommodate circumstances in which the values of relevant contextual parameters depart from those of the presumptive context.[61]

---

[61]To be sure, the difference between the context of conversation and that of published texts does not follow from any essential difference between writing and speech as modes of representation, but from the differences in the contexts in which each mode is typically used. Thus our characterization of the context of conversation would hold as well for direct, immediate written communication between individuals (skin divers writing

USES OF PARENTHETICALS

The various uses of the parenthetical can be classified along several dimensions. First, parentheticals vary according to the sorts of contextual variation that they accommodate, both in terms of the particular feature in which the alternate context departs from the presumptive one, and the properties of that feature that are presumed to be at variance from those of the presumed feature. Second, we can classify parentheticals according to the way in which their content is interpreted relative to the text: whether the content of the parenthetical is construed as applying to the situation described by the embedding text, or to the context in which the text is to be interpreted. With one class of parentheticals, we interpret the content as providing an alternate text, which is optimized relative to some context that departs from the presumptive context with respect to certain properties relative to interpretation. In (6.24) and (6.25), for example, the parentheticals make provision for readers who are less well familiar with the subject matter than the presumptive reader is assumed to be:

(6.24) He made his remarks to (then Secretary of State) Henry Kissinger.

(6.25) Several members were jailed for association with enemy (American) agents.

Thus in (6.24) we are enabled to construct an alternate text that contains the sentence *He made his remarks to then Secretary of State Henry Kissinger*, which addresses the needs of an alternate reader who, unlike the presumptive reader, does not know who Henry Kissinger was. Note that this class includes all of the "lexical" parentheticals that we discussed in chapter three, where the alternate text is constructed by a straightforward insertion of the the

---

instructions to one another on a blackboard, persons sitting at terminals and communicating via a real-time chat system); and at least a large part of our characterization of the context of public writing would hold as well of the context of a public radio broadcast.

parenthesized material into the linguistic context (that is, by an operation of "semantic erasure" of the parentheses themselves.) But text-category parentheticals may also serve the function of providing an alternate text, as in a sentence like (6.26), from a semantics textbook:

(6.26)   Among these will be the unit set (that is, the set with one member).

In this case, however, the syntactic algorithm for construction of the alternate text may be more complex; in (6.26), for example, we might best reconstruct the alternate text-sentence as *Among these will be the set with one member*, where a part of the content of the parenthetical is substituted for its antecedent in the presumptive text.

As examples (6.24)–(6.26) suggest, alternate-text parentheticals like these are often used to accommodate differences between the beliefs or interests of the presumptive reader and those of the alternate reader, though in some cases the discrepancy goes the other way, with the alternate reader presumed to know more about the subject, or to be more interested in it, than the presumptive reader is. Parentheticals of this sort are exemplified in (6.27) and (6.28):

(6.27)   But listening to his early recordings (which have just been re-issued by Angel). . .

(6.28)   The State in question is quite small (income about seven lakhs, area about 450 square miles), but notable owing to the high character and ability of its ruler.

This type is also used quite frequently in academic prose as a kind of back-and-fill maneuver by writers who are apprehensive about the reactions of the literal-minded reader, as in:

(6.29)   One answer might be that only different (sequences of) pitch directions count as different tones with respect to the inventory.

(6.30)   Clearly (any utterance of) the sentence *It is raining* will be true only if it is raining when the (utterance of the) sentence is spoken.

The implication here is something like "I presume that the ordinary reader will not require such a degree of precision, but I add this material as a sop to the picky-picky."

These parentheticals of elaboration shade imperceptibly into the "in case you're interested" parentheticals like those in (6.31)–(6.32):

(6.31)   The facts of her background include: . . .a beloved older brother who was institutionalized in his early 20s for "dementia praecox" (schizophrenia, probably) and died there some ten years later.

(6.32)   The next day we talked about his film (he speaks excellent English). . .

In these examples, however, it is probably not accurate to say that the material in the parenthetical addresses exclusively the interests of the alternate reader. Rather, it speaks to interests that the the author and reader might share if only the communicative purposes of the text were other than what is presupposed in the ideal case. These parentheticals are thus of the sort that might be described as "digressive," but it is important to keep in mind that one can reckon something a digression only relative to a prior determination of what would count as relevant, and that relevance is itself a contextually determined property of utterances. Thus the determination that a particular utterance or utterance-part is relevant can be made only in the light of prior assumptions about the conversational purposes and interests of the participants, which determine the point at issue.

As opposed to these alternate-text parentheticals, we can discern another class of "context-restriction" parentheticals, whose content is interpreted quite differently: as specifying the sub-class of contexts that are relevant to the interpretation of a particular text-expression. For example, consider a menu entry like (6.33):

(6.33)   Oysters (in season)

In the presumptive context, a typical restaurant menu is interpreted as a list of dishes that are available to the patron whenever he reads the menu under appropriate circumstances for ordering. In (6.33), the content of the parenthetical is interpreted as describing a more restricted class of contexts of interpretation in which this particular item is in fact available; i.e., "oysters are available if oysters are in season at the time the menu is (appropriately) presented to the customer" and so on. Parentheticals of this sort may also impose conditions on the physical circumstances of the context of interpretation, as in:

(6.34)   Season with salt (unless pork fat is cured), nutmeg, allspice and cayenne; mix in eggs.

(6.35)   How to connect your VCR to your cable box (for models without cable attachment)

It is notable that these examples, like many of this type, involve a text whose purpose is to serve as a basis for action (for example public signs, recipes, contracts, directions or menus), in which the described situation is more likely to be identical to the context of interpretation. (Perhaps for this reason, these uses of the parenthetical are not usually mentioned in standard handbook description, which are primarily concerned with narrative or expository genres.) Thus the steps of a menu are taken to describe an action that is to be performed by the interpreter in the context of interpretation, in which are present, presumably, all of the ingredients listed earlier; and the parenthetical "(unless pork fat is cured)" describes the narrower set of circumstances of interpretation in which the preceding action is to be performed.

Finally, note that the two types of parenthetical can also be combined, to provide an indication both of an alternate text and the context in which that text will provide the relevant interpretation. Consider (6.36), for example, from a credit-card application, or (6.37), from a menu:

(6.36)   APR 18% (12% in Ohio)

(6.37)   Add 1 tsp salt (1/2 tsp if pork fat is cured). . .

In these examples, the two components of the parenthetical are expressed as syntactically distinct expressions. Thus in (6.37) we conclude the expression *1/2 tsp* is to be substituted in the text for the phrase *1 tsp* just in case the context of interpretation is one in which the pork fact is cured. In other cases, however, the interpretation of such parentheticals may involve more complex reconstructions. Consider (6.38), for example, from a sign over an airport check-in counter:

(6.38)   CHECK IN (passengers with boarding passes may go directly to gate)

In (6.38), the parenthetical provides a substitute for the implicit instruction in the sign over the counter (i.e., "go to the gate" in place of "check in here"), and also indicates the alternate context in which the instruction is to be applied (i.e., one in which the addressee is a passenger with a boarding pass, rather than the presumptive addressee, who has none). But there is no simple syntactic mapping from the content of the parenthetical to the changes in the context and text that it stipulates, and the interpretation can be derived only through a fairly complex amalgamation of the content of the parenthetical with its embedding linguistic and extralinguistic environments.

Up to now I have discussed only examples of parentheticals that make provision for alternate circumstances of reading, that is, contexts in which either the addressee or the time, physical setting, or place of reading are different from those of the presumptive context. But of course parentheticals are also used to indicate cases in which the context of production departs from the presumptive case in such a way as to affect the interpretation. It is relatively rare that the writer will have to make any reference to variation in the time, place or physical circumstances of production, since these properties are known to him in advance of transmission of the document, and their effect can be accommodated in the course of transcription and revision of the text itself. (The exceptions most often involve ostensibly non-corrigible documents like letters or diaries, where a writer may use a parenthetical notation like "(two hours later)" or "(in a bumpy coach)" to describe features of the context that are relevant to the interpretation of the associated text.)

Most often, however, the features of the context of production that are relevant to interpretation will involve the author's intentions in inscribing the text, and will be construed as providing a kind of metalinguistic comment on the form or content of the associated antecedent. A paradigmatic instance is the sort of parenthetical found in (6.39) and (6.40):

(6.39)   Over and over again that kind of "spot of time" (in the Wordsworthian sense) was re-created for the reader in words just as it had been re-created for the narrator or central character in memory, accumulating a still greater freight of nostalgia and distance.

(6.40)   The first substance "polarizes" the light (in Malus's term) while the second analyzes it.

There is naturally a close association between these uses of parentheticals and the use of quotations. As we noted, quotations function essentially to mark a text-expression that is to be construed as having been produced in circumstances that differ from those of the surrounding text – or as we can describe it now, in a context that departs from the presumptive context of production. The parenthetical associated with the quoted material then provides a description of the relevant alternate context associated with the original production of the quoted expression (one, for example, in which the the author is speaking in a Wordsworthian voice). These uses are thus analogous to examples like *Season with salt (unless pork fat is cured)*, save that the parenthetical here describes the special features of the context of production, rather than those of the context of interpretation. By the same token, we often encounter "alternate-text" parentheticals of this type, which provide a substitute for the quoted phrase in question that would be appropriate to another context of production. Such parentheticals are generally associated with uses of quoted expressions for which the author wishes to provide an alternate in his own voice: for paraphrases, that is, of another writer's usage:

(6.41)   These "d-structure" (deep-structure) constraints. . .

And finally, as we might expect, we find mixed parentheticals like these, in which the parenthetical provides both an alternate text and an explicit indication of the context in which it was or would have been produced:

(6.42)   Over and over again that kind of telling moment (the "spot of time," as Wordsworth would have called it) was re-created for the reader. . . .

In this case, note that the quoted material falls within the parenthetical, as a gloss on the antecedent phrase. Here, that is, the parenthetical is construed as providing an alternate to the presumptive text as it might have been produced by a Wordsworthian speaker.

There are variations on this theme. Such parentheticals are used not only to comment on the form or provenance of a particular expression, but also on other circumstances surrounding its production, as in (6.43), where the parenthetical explains the contextual circumstances that motivate another to use an expression that the writer has quoted:

(6.43)   "Oh, my dears, what do you think? You'll never guess. A woman's been here asking me for her husband. Her *what*?" (Helen was fond of supplying her own surprise.) "Yes, for her husband, and it really is so." [E. M. Forster, *Howards End*]

But more importantly, writers use such parentheticals to remark their own states of mind with regard to their production of a particular expression, as in:[62]

---

[62]It is notable that these metalinguistic parentheticals are the first to be mastered by beginning writers, years before they even try to come to grips with those that make reference to a non-presumptive reader or interpretive setting. Thus a fifth-grader writes:

(*i*)   At lunch I played with Jonas. I killd him (pretend).

There is nothing surprising in this. A child is capable of monitoring and remarking upon his own production of language well before learning to write, and of reckoning the effect of his own intentions on the interpretation of an utterance, whereas there is nothing in the child's ordinary experience of spoken discourse that would enable him to anticipate the remote circumstances in which a written text will ultimately be interpreted, or the possibility of a non-presumptive reader.

(6.44)   Mr Kenge now retired and Richard with him, to where I was, near the door, leaving my pet (it is so natural to me [to call her thus] that again I can't help it!) sitting near the Lord Chancellor. . . [Dickens, *Bleak House*]

(6.45)   The songs on this LP, produced by Mitchell Froom, are often more inventively presented and even at times (dare we say) Beatlesque. [*People Magazine*]

At first consideration, some of these "production" parentheticals may appear to create a problem for the general account of parentheticals I have been developing here.   In the case of parentheticals that manifestly accommodate the possibility of alternate readers or circumstances of interpretation, we assume that the writer cannot know in advance whether the parenthetical will be relevant on any particular occasion of reading, but that the relevance will be apparent to the reader on that occasion.   That is what makes it possible to say that the content of the parenthetical is strictly irrelevant to the interpretation of the non-parenthesized text in the presumptive context, and so that the presumptive text can constitute a complete and integral communication.   Thus the content of the parenthetical in an example like "Check in (Passengers with boarding passes can proceed directly to gate)" can be simply ignored by the presumptive reader who does not have a boarding pass.   In the case of production parentheticals, however, it is not always clear why the relevance of the content of the parenthetical should depend on the circumstances of reading, or how the parenthetical can create two versions of a text.   Consider (6.46), for example:

(6.46)   Clocks may strike, suns rise and set, the moon herself accomplish an entire revolution, but the loftier enterprises of man have always ignored such promptings.   What is time?   And, after all (I thought), why should the Exhibition not be opened in a day or two.   It is open even now.   [E. M. Forster "Our Diversions"]

Suppose we were to assume that the non-parenthesized text in (6.46) is complete in the presumptive context of interpretation; that is, that it can be assigned a coherent interpretation without reference to the content of the parenthetical. Then we must explain under what non-presumptive circumstances of reading the parenthetical would be required for interpretation: why information about the internal state of the writer at the time of production should make a difference to some readers but not to others. On the other hand, suppose the non-parenthesized text in (6.46) is *not* complete in the presumptive context of interpretation: that is, that the presumptive reader will arrive at a pernicious misreading of the text if he does not ascribe the content of the embedding sentence to the writer's thoughts at a time prior to inscription, rather than at the moment of inscription. In that case, we must abandon the general account of parentheticals presented here, which depends crucially on the assumption that parentheticals are not properly part of the presumptive text. (What is more, we will then have to explain why production parentheticals like these are subject to the same sorts of syntactic restrictions as the others, the observation that originally motivated this analysis.)

This difficulty can be resolved in two stages. Strictly (that is, semantically) speaking, the unparenthesized text associated with production parentheticals *is* interpretively complete in the presumptive context, in the sense that it must yield a coherent interpretation independent of the content of the associated parenthetical. Thus a parenthetical alone cannot license the wholly non-standard use of a term, as in:[63]

---

[63]Note that the use of quotation marks around a phrase may help to mark it as a non-standard use of an expression ("as someone would say") so long as some appropriate interpretation is recoverable from its form alone; but this device is not sufficient to redeem the relevant usages in (*i*) or (*ii*) which are ill-formed because the presumptive reader could not be expected to supply a sense for the quoted expressions without recourse to the information contained in the parentheticals:

(*i*)   ??Bush seems to me a kind of "Uncle Arthur" (I have in mind my mother's brother, who usually seemed competent, but had a tendency to blow a crucial circuit at moments of particular stress).

(*ii*)   ??The United States is actually a highly "communist" society (in the sense in which the term was used by certain of the little-studied Czech communards of the 1850's).

(6.47)   ??Bush seems to me a kind of Uncle Arthur (I have in mind my mother's brother, who usually seemed competent, but had a tendency to blow a crucial circuit at moments of particular stress).

(6.48)   Bush seems to me to be a kind of Uncle Arthur – I have in mind my mother's brother, who usually seemed competent, but had a tendency to blow a crucial circuit at moments of particular stress.

(6.49)   ??The United States is actually a highly communist society (in the sense in which the term was used by certain of the little-studied Czech communards of the 1850's).

(6.50)   The United States is actually a highly communist society, in the sense in which the term was used by certain of the little-studied Czech communards of the 1850's.

When we encounter a sentence like (6.51), then, we interpret the content of the parenthetical as an elaboration that specifies the source of the relevant wording as might be required by the interests of a specialized reader, but as not essential to the interpretation of the presumptive text:

(6.51)   Over and over again that kind of "spot of time" (in the Wordsworthian sense) was re-created for the reader in words. . .

But in other cases it appears more difficult to draw such a distinction between a presumptive reader who is not interested in the content of the parenthetical and a non-presumptive reader who is interested, at least if we define these presumptive elements extensionally; that is, as different individuals. For example, when a reviewer for *People Magazine* says, "The songs are . . .(dare we say?) Beatlesque," he surely does not intend that some of his readers will ignore the parenthetical while others will take it to heart. Note that the problem is not restricted to parentheticals that refer to the circumstances of production; it affects the great majority of the uses of parentheticals in literary texts (by which I mean roughly texts in which irony may be appropriate); for example:

(6.52)   Away and away the aeroplane shot, till it was nothing but a bright spark; an aspiration; a concentration; a symbol (so it seemed to Mr. Bentley, vigorously rolling his strip of turf at Greenwich) of man's soul. . . [Virginia Woolf, *Mrs. Dalloway*]

(6.53)   Fog everywhere. Fog up the river, where it flows among green aits and meadows; fog down the river, where it rolls defiled among the tiers of shipping and the waterside pollutions of a great (and dirty) city. [Dickens, *Bleak House*]

(6.54)   He was shabby and work-stained, but the observant eye would have noted an idea in his dress (his appearance was plainly not a matter of indifference to himself), and a painter (not of the heroic) would have liked to make a sketch of him. [James, *The Princess Casamassima*]

The parenthetical in (6.52) describes the context of production of the associated expression (more precisely, the point of view from which the observation is offered); but the parentheticals in (6.53) and (6.54) would be better described as parentheticals of elaboration; that is, parentheticals that supply information over and above what is required by the interests or background of the presumptive reader. But how can this be, when it is quite clear that Dickens and James intend that the parentheticals shall be read and interpreted by all readers? Surely it would be wrong to say that it would be possible to construct a "complete" reading of a text of *Bleak House* or *The Princess Casamassima* from which all parenthesized elements had been deleted.

The solution to the dilemma involves a reformulation of what exactly we intend when we speak of presumptive and non-presumptive elements of the context. As I noted earlier in connection with the example from *Huckleberry Finn* ("You don't know about me without you have read a book by the name of *The Adventures of Tom Sawyer*; but that ain't no matter"), the presumptive reader is itself a construct that actual readers must define, and with whom they must identify in the process of interpretation of the text. In the case of a literary text, the author may have in mind several such readers, which are no less the writer's own constructs than the characters or the narrative personae for which he is more plainly responsible.   Thus to take an example discussed by Raymond Williams, Burke's *Reflections on the Revolution in France* is written as if in the form of an open letter to to a young French gentleman, but is clearly intended for the edification of Burke's countrymen; and in reading the text, we must identify ourselves with (our reconstructions of) both the ostensible addressee and the actual audience. More generally, it has been variously suggested that any ironic discourse requires the postulation of both an innocent addressee and a knowing audience.[64] When someone says ironically "She's a fine friend," for example, we recover the ironic effect by juxtaposing our own disbelief with the credulity of an innocent addressee who would construe the remark literally (and with whom, moreover, we may identify our earlier selves).

It is dissociations of this sort that provide the occasions for the literary use of parentheticals. When Dickens refers to London as "a great (and dirty) city," he makes as if to address his primary text to a complacent addressee who prefers to remain ignorant of the pollutions of the city; the parenthetical accommodates the interests of another reader who is willing to acknowledge the repugnant side of familiar things. In the course of interpretation, the actual reader identifies himself with both roles, but they are not quite parallel. One is what we may call the "putative presumptive reader," the other the "presumptive listener-on."

Not all literary uses of parentheticals resolve themselves after just this pattern, but all of them can be explained through the multiplication and complication of second-person constructs. In the following example from Virginia Woolf's *Mrs. Dalloway*, for example, the putative addressee and listener-on are further

---

[64]The most lapidary version of this view is given by Fowler (1926): "Irony is a form of utterance that postulates a double audience, consisting of one party that hearing shall hear & that hearing shall not understand, & another party that, when more is meant than meets the ear, is aware both of that more & of the outsiders' incomprehension." For a systematic exposition of this view of irony, see Clark and Gerrig (1984).

associated with distinct personae in the interior monologue of the subject, as rendered in free indirect discourse:

(6.56)   ¶For having lived in Westminster—how many years now? over twenty,—one feels even in the midst of the traffic, or waking at night, Clarissa was positive, a particular hush, or solemnity; an indescribable pause; a suspense (but that might be her heart, affected, they said, by influenza) before Big Ben strikes. There! *Mrs. Dalloway*[65]

Examples like these are far too complicated to pick over here, and in any event are irrelevant to our philistine purposes. For us, these literary examples serve primarily to show how the parenthetical is intimately connected to the nature of public writing. It has become an important tenet of recent literary theory that modern literary discourse (as an instance of written public discourse in general) defines itself in the complex relationships it establishes between writers and their audience, and in particular in the invention of "the reader" as a particular kind of social construct. It should not be surprising that the parenthetical, which arose as a practical device for dealing with various indeterminacies in the context of public discourse, should come to be used as a means of exploiting these circumstances in the service of literary expression.

THE INTEGRATION OF FUNCTIONAL CATEGORIES AND A
HISTORICAL POSTSCRIPT

As with the parenthetical, we can see how the other text-grammatical categories we have mentioned are either dedicated or adapted to the particular circumstances of public writing. For example, it has been argued that the explicit indication of direct quotation is a feature particularly appropriate to the uses of printed texts, where the original wording of a source can be presumed to be reliably

---

[65]Note that this passage manifests a practice in which dashes do not absorb commas (and usually, in which dashes are not themselves absorbed by semicolons and colons), a style that was common with many publishers until the early years of this century.

preserved in a number of identical exemplars.[66] By the same token, the hierarchical information provided by argument-structure categories like the sentence and paragraph is particularly useful for the presentation of the sorts of long and complex disquisitions that are characteristic of written traditions.

Note however that each of these functions answers to a distinct and in principle separable property of public writing. Thus the usefulness of writing as a means of recording complicated narratives and arguments is in great measure independent of its means of publication and dissemination, which are the characteristics most relevant to the use of contextual categories like quotations and parentheticals. By the same token, it would seem as if there should be no necessary connection between the text units that are relevant to argument structure, and those that are relevant to special circumstances in the context of interpretation or of production. By way of analogy, we can consider the relation between quotation and the constituent structures determined by lexical grammar. By and large, we note that quotations can ignore lexical constituencies; constraints are more often stylistic than syntactic:

(6.57)   That night, she said, they "tried to sneak up on the rat" who was "messing around with" her friends "and kinfolks."

(6.58)   Given these revelations, the assemblyman said, he "wouldn't be surprised if" the committee reports that "the feds have been tapping the phones of a whole bunch of" Democratic legislators.

Yet at the same time, we have already noted that the domains of contextual categories are interdefined with those of argument-structure categories by complex syntactic dependencies. Quotations offer perhaps the best example of these dependencies, since there seems to be no functional reason why the distribution of quotations should correlate in any interesting way with the boundaries of categories like the text-sentence. For example, we note that a quotation, like a parenthetical, cannot in general straddle a sentence-boundary:

---

[66]For discussion, see Eisenstein (1979).

(6.59)   *Nor would he consider trying to join Leslie and his men, rumoured to be close at hand and making for Scotland, "which I thought to be absolutely impossible. I decided instead to make for France," where it was hoped that Louis would back the royalist cause.

There is one apparent exception to this generalization: a quotation initiated (or terminated) by a sentence-internal phase may be continued by a number of further quoted sentences:

(6.60)   Yet Craig remains confident that the pitching "will come 'round sooner or later. We just have to hope everybody stays healthy."

At first glance, this example appears to suggest that quotations and text-sentences can have overlapping constituencies, as in

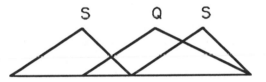

(with the proviso that the quotation must coincide at one end or the other with a sentence-boundary, so as to disallow a sentence like (6.59)). There is reason, however, for assuming that sentences like (6.60) in fact result from a rule that allows omission of sequences of opening and closing quotes between utterances produced by the same speaker, when there is no intervening punctuation. Note for example that such "quotation splices" are odd when the internal quotation terminates with a question mark:

(6.61)   *I still have questions: what did he know, and when, as the committee chairman put it, "did it suddenly pop into his head to remember it? You'd think he would have given us an answer to that one."

where if the external question mark would presumably not be transposed, and the conditions for quotation mark omission would not be satisfied.[67]

We can offer analogous observations about the behavior of parentheticals. On purely functional grounds, for example, there is no reason why a sentence-internal parenthetical of elaboration should not itself contain more than one text-sentence, as in (6.62):

(6.62)   *He complained that the book was too long (it goes on for 1048 pages. Two hundred and forty pages are spent on Nelson's childhood alone).

In fact there are styles that allow this construction, but it is ungrammatical in modern American English.[68] These restrictions on

---

[67]In this connection, note also that this construction is not used in British English in circumstances when the period on the embedding sentence would not be imported:

(i)   Melbourne had dismissed Dickens's *Oliver Twist* as 'all about Workhouses, and Coffin Makers, and Pickpockets'. 'I don't like that low and debasing view of mankind.' [Asa Briggs, *A Social History of England*]

where the two quoted expressions are in fact contiguous in the original source.

[68]Some British usage appears to allow this construction (which is analogous to the "straddling" quotations we mentioned in the previous note), as in the following examples:

(i)   With various delicate transitions that left me sighing in assent, the film now turned into a gentle, parodic love story, the girl civilizing Spunk – teaching him how to dress, eat, speak – and Spunk decivilizing her: teaching her to kick the booze, the pick-ups, the self-destruction, the money (they go primitive for a while, after Spunk has an urban breakdown. Even I, in my exalted state, could detect some sentimentality here). [Martin Amis, *Money*]

(ii)   The Tory party has been called the stupid party (and not unfairly, to be stupid and to be sensible are not far apart. The Progressive party, Radical and Socialist, is clever, but silly). [A.J.P. Taylor, "Lord Salisbury"] the use of quotations and parentheticals must therefore be laid to the structure of the text-grammar itself, which specifies the circumstances under which categories like quotations and parentheticals can be introduced as text-sentential and text-clausal constituents.

Observations like these underscore the point that the text-grammar does not simply provide a repertory of functional categories that can be used to mark expressions according to the role they play in the structure and contextual interpretation of the text. It also constitutes a systematic framework for the syntactic and presentational integration of these functions, and as a system, is more highly constrained than a consideration of the functions of any of its elements, taken separately, would require. (Among other things, this entails that there are semantically coherent combinations of text-categories of which the text-grammar does not allow expression.) For this reason we can conclude that the text-sentence serves not just as a classifier of argument structure, but as the integral unit of composition and processing of natural-language text.

In American English, these sentences would have to be rewritten with semicolons doing the work of the parenthetical-internal periods, perhaps with some rhetorical differences.

7 CONCLUSION

The outline of text-grammar that I have offered here suggests a number of directions for further research, but I will conclude by bringing up two historical questions. Why did the text-grammar arise when it did, and why is it important to writing? I mentioned earlier that there was good reason for saying that the text-sentence did not emerge as a grammatical category until some time after the introduction of print. In her survey of punctuation in the scribal tradition, Levinson (1986) suggests that we can begin to identify text-sentences (or as she calls them "orthographic" sentences) in the seventeenth century, and I am inclined to agree with this date. Even in early seventeenth-century texts, however, the detection and interpretation of what would now be sentence boundaries is not always easy. Levinson cites these examples:

(7.1)　　But then I reasoned againe, Christ was both God and man , therefore hee coulde withstand the terrors of death :but I am a fleshly man, and perhance I cannot vndergoone the cruell pangs of death:but my conscience solved all this doubt,in that the Martyrs were fleshly man,and siners , yet by the grace of God were strengthened to die, therefore by the same grace shall I be sustained. And in this cogitation I was much comfoorted and prevailed in spirit,&wholly gave my selfe over to suffer death:and they lead me streight waies to the place of execution ,and bound me hand, and foot in maner of a corpse upon the earth, as apeareth by this figure. (1617)

(7.2)   . . .you are to impute the Error to the absence of the Author, Whose affaires in the Country tooke him from cares of the City:or too explaine himselfe more fully, that he may come off fairley; and possesse him of your opinion more freely; he was called away. . .(1630)

But whenever the text-sentence can be said to have made its official debut, certainly there is no analogous unit in the syntax of medieval and Renaissance texts. This has sometimes been a source of frustration to editors and critics concerned with normalizing and interpreting texts from this period. For example, Levinson quotes critics commenting on various early Renaissance writers as follows:

> Lydgate's sense of syntax was. . .uncertain. . . He has no rules to guide him in the construction of the sentences; indeed he often seems to start out with no clear idea of where his sentence will lead him.

> A new sentence almost always means a new paragraph, for Peacock's sentence is a segmented thing that crawls over the page and often may be divided into self-sustaining units. It is annoying to find a whole section which is too loose to be transcribed as one sentence and too involved to be separated.

> [Malory's] syntax is often, by modern standards, regrettably loose; but though many of the sentences would be hard to parse, their meaning is usually clear.

But as Levinson points out, these critics err in imputing "sentences" to the texts in question, for although sentence-like indicators are used in these texts, the units they mark do not correspond either functionally or syntactically to the modern text-sentence. As Levinson puts it, these writers simply did not write in sentences. This should not be taken as evidence of unclear or disorganized thought or language, as the critics cited here have done. Lydgate and Malory were in full control of the lexical grammar of their language, and we can discern a fairly rigorous conceptual structure in their argumentation. They simply did not have available a conventionalized system of explicit categorical organization that they could impose on their texts to signal the kinds of structural and contextual information that we now consider necessary to the interpretation of texts in genres like the ones they wrote in. And in the absence of such a system, they were not constrained to organize their texts according to the sorts of constraints that the text-grammar imposes, whereby the functions of various sub-sentential units must be subordinated to a set of structural patterns that make it possible to treat the sentence as a unit of composition and processing.

For this reason it is not possible to "modernize" the punctuation of these texts in a manner faithful to their original sense (though such modernization has become the standard practice even for texts in which authentic spellings are preserved, and whose purely pedagogical usefulness is therefore questionable). The practice of modernization in fact involves a mistaken assumption about modern punctuation: that punctuation marks informational units and relations in a neutral way, and hence should be applicable to any text that is coherently organized on independent grounds. It is this misconception that underlies the critics' frustration with manuscript sources, the assumption being that the failure of such texts to yield up a structure that can be regimented according to modern text-categories must be an indication of a lack of clarity or organizational rigor in the original. Whereas I have tried to show that the defining characteristic of the grammar is the way in which it constrains and integrates the distribution of text-categories over and above what their informational functions, interpreted severally, would require.

Why did such a system evolve, and what were the immediate circumstances that made it possible? As usual in discussions of such matters, we can only point to a cluster of interconnected observations and developments, without being able to arrange them decisively according to their places in a chain of carts and horses. But certainly the introduction of print had a lot to do with the establishment of the system. We have already noted that the mechanics of distribution of print materials create the communicative need for systematic conventions for the marking of certain text-categories, such as the parenthetical and many uses of the quotation. But over and above the particular communicative requirements that printed texts impose on the writer and reader, the process of printing makes the development of the text-grammar both possible and desirable. For one thing, print abets all aspects of the process of language standardization, by making available a set of uniform exemplars of written texts that are commonly known to be available to a wide community. Then too, print (together with other things) fostered the development of a larger literate class, and of an increase in the uses and cultural importance of written material. Over the course of time, as has been variously suggested, this led in turn to the development of a written-language grammar, as well as of conventions of typography and design, that make for more efficient, more highly "readable" texts – particularly as the process of silent reading became more common (probably a seventeenth- or eighteenth-century development). Finally, all of these factors conspired to redefine traditional genres, and to create new ones, which presupposed new principles of organization and new relationships between the writer and reader, and so in turn required the introduction of more highly constrained schemes of text organization. For example the formal linguistic properties that classical theorists associated with the definitions of genres, such as meter, stanzaic form and "level" of language, could now be replaced or augmented with conventions pertaining to the physical form of inscription, which was obviously impossible in a scribal tradition.[69] Thus by the eighteenth century, Sterne could play parodically with the punctuational and graphical conventions of the novel in *Tristram Shandy* in just the way that a poet a century earlier might have played with the metrical and stanzaic conventions of pastoral elegy.

It would be an ambitious undertaking to trace the structural history of the text-grammar of English or some other developed language, and to sort out the external influences that shaped its development. One thing is certain, however: the elaboration of the text-grammar went hand-in-hand with the development of the particular "periodic voice" which has underlain all of English prose since the seventeenth century (and which has analogues in all other intellectualized European languages as well). By way of ostensive

---

[69]In this connection, let me stress that it is a mistake to consider the development of the text-grammar independently of the development of the ancillary genre-specific conventions (for example, for footnoting) and corollary graphical systems (for example, for charts and tables), with which it has been inextricably connected.

demonstration of this point, here are some examples from, respectively, an eighteenth-century historian, a nineteenth-century novelist, a twentieth-century novelist, and finally, from a twentieth-century grammarian:

(7.3)   The Goths were now in possession of the Ukraine, a country of considerable extent and uncommon fertility, intersected with navigable rivers which, from either side, discharge themselves into the Borysthenes ; and interspersed with large and lofty forests of oaks. The plenty of game and fish, the innumerable bee-hives, deposited in the hollows of old trees, and in the cavities of rocks, and forming, even in that rude age, a valuable branch of commerce, the size of the cattle, the temperature of the air, the aptness of the soil for every species of grain, and the luxuriancy of the vegetation, all displayed the liberality of Nature, and tempted the industry of man.   But the Goths withstood all these temptations, and still adhered to a life of idleness, of poverty, and of rapine. [Gibbon, *Decline and Fall of the Roman Empire*, Ch. X]

(7.4)   Pen trolled over some verses he had been making that morning, in which he informed himself that the woman who had slighted his passion could not be worthy to win it: that he was awaking from love's mad fever, and, of course, under these circumstances, proceeded to leave her, and to quit a heartless deceiver: that a name which had one day been famous in the land, might again be heard in it: and, that though he should never be the happy and careless boy he was but a few months since, or his heart be what it had been ere passion had filled it and grief had well-nigh killed it; that though to him personally death was as welcome as life, and that he would not hesitate to part with the latter, but for the love of one kind being whose happiness depended on his own, – yet he hoped to show he was a man worthy of his race, and that one day the false one should be brought to know how great was the treasure and noble the heart which she had flung away. [Thackeray, *The History of Pendennis*, Ch XIV]

(7.5)   Jeremy Bentham's stuffed body would not have been ill at ease in their house. You went into a warm dark cozy morass or limbo of fire-dogs, dough-chests (full of old numbers of the *Journal of Social Psychology*), Delft pepper-mills, needle-point footstools, barometers, chess-tables, candle-molds, Holbeins (their motto was, *If it isn't a Holbein, it isn't a picture*—and Dr. Whitaker himself looked like a Holbein of the aged Emile), quilts, counterpanes, comforters, throws, Afghans, stoles (that had got in among the others by mistake), hooked, knitted, quilted, tied, crocheted, and appliqued rugs—my favorite was a Pennsylvania Dutch one with some sort of animal on it and underneath, in German, *Don't Tread on Me*. [Randall Jarrell, *Pictures from an Institution*]

(7.6)   Subordinate clauses are sentences containing a subject and predicate, but serving the purpose in the main sentence (to which they are joined sometimes by a subordinating conjunction or relative pronoun, but sometimes without any separate and visible link) of single words, namely, of noun, adjective or adverb; they are called respectively substantival, adjectival or adverbial clauses. [H. W. Fowler and F. G. Fowler, *The King's English*]

These passages are so manifestly different in tone and purpose that there are few points of view from which they can be more profitably compared than contrasted; yet each in its way exemplifies the absolute dependence of modern prose on the text-grammatical apparatus I have described here, which regiments the written expression of ideas according to the patterns it provides, and permits the construction of elements of discourse that are different both in kind and degree from anything that would be made available by a bare system for the transcription of spoken-language intonation.

REFERENCES

Anderson, Stephen. 1974. *The Organization of Phonology*. New York: Academic Press.

Biber, Douglas. 1986. Spoken and Written Textual Dimensions of English. *Language* 62:2.384–414.

Bloomfield, Leonard. 1933. *Language*. New York: Henry Holt.

Bolinger, Dwight. 1975. *Aspects of Language*. New York: Harcourt Brace Jovanovich.

Carey, G. V. 1952. *Mind the Stop*. Cambridge: Cambridge University Press.

Chafe, Wallace L. 1982. Integration and Involvement in Speaking, Writing, and Oral Literature, in D. Tannen, ed. *Spoken and Written Language*. Norwood, New Jersey: Ablex.

Chafe, Wallace L. and Jane Danielewicz. 1985. Properties of Spoken and Written Language, in Rosalind Horowitz and S. J. Samuels, eds. *Comprehending Oral and Written Language*. New York: Academic Press.

Clark, Herbert H. and Richard J. Gerrig. 1984. On the Pretense Theory of Irony. *Journal of Experimental Psychology* 113:1.121–126.

Cruttenden, Alan. 1986. *Intonation*. Cambridge: Cambridge University Press.

Culy, Christopher D. (ms). Cookbook Linguistics: Recipes and Linguistic Theory.

Eisenstein, Elizabeth. 1979. *The Printing Press as an Agent of Change*. Cambridge: Cambridge University Press.

Emonds, Joseph E. 1976. *A Transformational Approach to English Syntax*. New York: Academic Press.

Fillmore, Charles. 1975. Santa Cruz Lectures on Deixis 1971, circulated by Indiana University Linguistics Club.

Fowler, Henry Watson. 1926. *Dictionary of Modern English Usage*. Oxford: Clarendon.

Fowler, Henry Watson and Francis George Fowler. 1931. *The King's English*. Oxford: Oxford University Press.

Gleason, Henry Allan. 1965. *Linguistics and English Grammar*. New York: Holt, Rinehart and Winston.

Kroch, Anthony S. and Donald Hindle. 1982. A Quantitative Study of the Syntax of Speech and Writing. Final report to the National Institute of Education.

Levinson, Joan. 1986. Punctuation and the Orthographic Sentence: a Linguistic Analysis. City University of New York dissertation.

Lowth, Robert. 1762. *A Short Introduction to English Grammar*. (Scolar Press facsimile, Menston, England, 1967).

Marckwardt, Albert H. 1942. *Introduction to the English Language*. New York: Oxford University Press.

McCawley, James. (ms). Linguistic Aspects of Two Non-linguistic Notational Frameworks.

McCawley, James. 1982. Parentheticals and Discontinuous Constituent Structure. *Linguistic Inquiry* 13:1.91–106.

Meyer, Charles F. 1983. A Descriptive Study of American Punctuation. University of Wisconsin dissertation.

Meyer, Charles F. 1987. *A Linguistic Study of American Punctuation*. New York: Peter Lang.

Mountford, John. 1980. Writing System as a Concept in Linguistics. *Information Design Journal*, 1:4.223–231.

Norrish, Patricia. 1987. *The Graphic Translatability of Text*. British Library R & D Report 5854. Reading, England: Department of Typography and Graphic Communication, University of Reading.

Ong, Walter J. 1987. The Writer's Audience is Always a Fiction, in Vassilis Lambropoulos and David Neal Miller, eds. *Twentieth-Century Literary Theory*. Albany: State University of New York Press.

Partridge, Eric. 1953. *You Have a Point There*. London: Routledge & Kegan Paul.

Rubin, Andee. 1980. A Theoretical Taxonomy of the Differences between Oral and Written Languages, in Rand J. Spiro, et al., eds. *Theoretical Issues in Reading Comprehension*. Hillsdale, New Jersey: Erlbaum.

Sampson, Geoffrey. 1985. *Writing Systems*. Stanford: Stanford University Press.

Smith, Brian. 1987. The Correspondence Continuum. Report No. CSLI–87–71, Center for the Study of Language and Information.

Sumney, G. 1949. *Modern Punctuation*. New York: The Ronald Press.

Whitehall, Harold. 1954. *Structural Essentials of English*. New York: Harcourt Brace and Company.

INDEX

CSLI Publications

Reports

The following titles have been published in the CSLI Reports series. These reports may be obtained from CSLI Publications, Ventura Hall, Stanford University, Stanford, CA 94305-4115.

The Situation in Logic–I Jon Barwise CSLI–84–2 ($2.00)

Coordination and How to Distinguish Categories Ivan Sag, Gerald Gazdar, Thomas Wasow, and Steven Weisler CSLI–84–3 ($3.50)

Belief and Incompleteness Kurt Konolige CSLI–84–4 ($4.50)

Equality, Types, Modules and Generics for Logic Programming Joseph Goguen and José Meseguer CSLI–84–5 ($2.50)

Lessons from Bolzano Johan van Benthem CSLI–84–6 ($1.50)

Self-propagating Search: A Unified Theory of Memory Pentti Kanerva CSLI–84–7 ($9.00)

Reflection and Semantics in LISP Brian Cantwell Smith CSLI–84–8 ($2.50)

The Implementation of Procedurally Reflective Languages Jim des Rivières and Brian Cantwell Smith CSLI–84–9 ($3.00)

Parameterized Programming Joseph Goguen CSLI–84–10 ($3.50)

Shifting Situations and Shaken Attitudes Jon Barwise and John Perry CSLI–84–13 ($4.50)

Completeness of Many-Sorted Equational Logic Joseph Goguen and José Meseguer CSLI–84–15 ($2.50)

Moving the Semantic Fulcrum Terry Winograd CSLI–84–17 ($1.50)

On the Mathematical Properties of Linguistic Theories C. Raymond Perrault CSLI–84–18 ($3.00)

A Simple and Efficient Implementation of Higher-order Functions in LISP Michael P. Georgeff and Stephen F. Bodnar CSLI–84–19 ($4.50)

On the Axiomatization of "if-then-else" Irène Guessarian and José Meseguer CSLI–85–20 ($3.00)

The Situation in Logic–II: Conditionals and Conditional Information Jon Barwise CSLI–84–21 ($3.00)

Principles of OBJ2 Kokichi Futatsugi, Joseph A. Goguen, Jean-Pierre Jouannaud, and José Meseguer CSLI–85–22 ($2.00)

Querying Logical Databases Moshe Vardi CSLI–85–23 ($1.50)

Computationally Relevant Properties of Natural Languages and Their Grammar Gerald Gazdar and Geoff Pullum CSLI–85–24 ($3.50)

An Internal Semantics for Modal Logic: Preliminary Report Ronald Fagin and Moshe Vardi CSLI–85–25 ($2.00)

The Situation in Logic–III: Situations, Sets and the Axiom of Foundation Jon Barwise CSLI–85–26 ($2.50)

Semantic Automata Johan van Benthem CSLI–85–27 ($2.50)

Restrictive and Non-Restrictive Modification Peter Sells CSLI–85–28 ($3.00)

Institutions: Abstract Model Theory for Computer Science J. A. Goguen and R. M. Burstall CSLI–85–30 ($4.50)

A Formal Theory of Knowledge and Action Robert C. Moore CSLI–85–31 ($5.50)

Finite State Morphology: A Review of Koskenniemi (1983) Gerald Gazdar CSLI–85–32 ($1.50)

The Role of Logic in Artificial Intelligence Robert C. Moore CSLI–85–33 ($2.00)

Events and "Logical Form" Stephen Neale CSLI–88–113 ($2.00)

Backwards Anaphora and Discourse Structure: Some Considerations Peter Sells CSLI–87–114 ($2.50)

Toward a Linking Theory of Relation Changing Rules in LFG Lori Levin CSLI–87–115 ($4.00)

Fuzzy Logic L. A. Zadeh CSLI–88–116 ($2.50)

Dispositional Logic and Commonsense Reasoning L. A. Zadeh CSLI–88–117 ($2.00)

Intention and Personal Policies Michael Bratman CSLI–88–118 ($2.00)

Unification and Agreement Michael Barlow CSLI–88–120 ($2.50)

Extended Categorial Grammar Suson Yoo and Kiyong Lee CSLI–88–121 ($4.00)

Unaccusative Verbs in Dutch and the Syntax-Semantics Interface Annie Zaenen CSLI–88–123 ($3.00)

What Is Unification? A Categorical View of Substitution, Equation and Solution Joseph A. Goguen CSLI–88–124 ($3.50)

Types and Tokens in Linguistics Sylvain Bromberger CSLI–88–125 ($3.00)

Determination, Uniformity, and Relevance: Normative Criteria for Generalization and Reasoning by Analogy Todd Davies CSLI–88–126 ($4.50)

Modal Subordination and Pronominal Anaphora in Discourse Craige Roberts CSLI–88–127 ($4.50)

The Prince and the Phone Booth: Reporting Puzzling Beliefs Mark Crimmins and John Perry CSLI–88–128 ($3.50)

Set Values for Unification-Based Grammar Formalisms and Logic Programming William Rounds CSLI–88–129 ($4.00)

Fifth Year Report of the Situated Language Research Program CSLI–88–130 (free)

Locative Inversion in Chicheŵa: A Case Study of Factorization in Grammar Joan Bresnan and Jonni M. Kanerva CSLI–88–131 ($5.00)

An Information-Based Theory of Agreement Carl Pollard and Ivan A. Sag CSLI–88–132 ($4.00)

Relating Models of Polymorphism José Meseguer CSLI–88–133 ($4.50)

Psychology, Semantics, and Mental Events under Descriptions Peter Ludlow CSLI–89–135 ($3.50)

Mathematical Proofs of Computer System Correctness Jon Barwise CSLI–89–136 ($3.50)

The X-bar Theory of Phrase Structure András Kornai and Geoffrey K. Pullum CSLI–89–137 ($4.00)

Discourse Structure and Performance Efficiency in Interactive and Noninteractive Spoken Modalities Sharon L. Oviatt and Philip R. Cohen CSLI–90–138 ($5.50)

The Contributing Influence of Speech and Interaction on Some Aspects of Human Discourse Sharon L. Oviatt and Philip R. Cohen CSLI–90–139 ($3.50)

The Connectionist Construction of Concepts Adrian Cussins CSLI–90–140 ($6.00)

Sixth Year Report CSLI–90–141 (free)

Lecture Notes

The titles in this series are distributed by the University of Chicago Press and may be purchased in academic or university bookstores or ordered directly from the distributor at 5801 Ellis Avenue, Chicago, Illinois 60637.

A Manual of Intensional Logic Johan van Benthem, second edition, revised and expanded. Lecture Notes No. 1

Emotion and Focus Helen Fay Nissenbaum. Lecture Notes No. 2

Lectures on Contemporary Syntactic Theories Peter Sells. Lecture Notes No. 3

Other CSLI Titles Distributed by UCP

Books Distributed by CSLI

Titles distributed by CSLI may be
ordered directly from CSLI Publications, Ventura Hall, Stanford University, Stanford, California 94305-4115.